Leadership and Environmental Stewardship

A Curriculum for Camps and Other Youth Programs

Barry A. Garst, Ph.D.
American Camp Association

Christine P. White, M.S.
National FFA Organization

HEALTHY LEARNING™
www.healthylearning.com

ISBN: 978-1-60679-211-7
Library of Congress Control Number: 2012932691
Cover design: Roger W. Rybkowski
Book layout: Roger W. Rybkowski
Front cover photo: Jon Beard

Healthy Learning
P.O. Box 1828
Monterey, CA 93942
www.healthylearning.com

Acknowledgments

This book is based on Camp 2 Grow, a national leadership and environmental stewardship program developed by the American Camp Association® (ACA) through funding from Lilly Endowment, Inc. to teach youth fundamental leadership knowledge and skills as well as provide youth with a framework for implementing environmental stewardship applications in their camps, homes, schools, and communities. Camp 2 Grow was implemented in U.S. day and resident camps from 2009 through 2011. The authors recognize the National FFA Organization's important contribution to this book through the selected LifeKnowledge® leadership lessons used as source material. LifeKnowledge is a collection of more than 200 lesson plans for developing the soft skills of leadership, personal growth, and career success. LifeKnowledge was created by National FFA when a team of more than 1,000 teachers, researchers, and professionals comprehensively defined leadership and the competencies that make up leadership attributes.

Special thanks to Lilly Endowment, Inc. for its support for the Camp 2 Grow program and to the participating camps that implemented Camp 2 Grow from 2009 through 2011.

The authors also recognize the involvement of the following individuals who contributed to the success of Camp 2 Grow and the completion of this book: Deb Bialeschki, Ph.D., Chris Chavez, Laurie Brown, Ph.D., and Jenna Genson, M.S.

Contents

1

Using This Book

"Tell me and I'll forget.
Show me and I may remember.
Involve me and I'll understand."
—Chinese proverb

Introduction

Nature and Youth

Nature is important for healthy child development (Kellert, 2005; Taylor et al., 2006). Getting kids outside and active promotes a healthy lifestyle that is essential to fighting obesity and reducing symptoms associated with attention deficit disorder, depression, and stress (Moore & Cooper Marcus, 2008; Trudeau & Shephard, 2008). Over the past decade, a movement has developed to "reconnect" children and nature. The foundation of this growing movement has been grounded in a belief that children are increasingly losing meaningful contact with the natural world in favor of extended time indoors—time often spent in front of an assortment of television, computer, and mobile device screens (Charles & Louv, 2009; Louv, 2005).

Experiences in nature are important for stewardship. Researchers have found that people with stronger emotional connections to nature demonstrate more environmentally responsible beliefs and behaviors (Kals, Schumacher, & Montada, 1999; Arnold, Cohen, & Warner, 2009; Chawla, 1999). In other words, kids who learn to care about nature are motivated to take care of nature. Within the movement to connect children and nature, a growing sentiment suggests that if children fail to develop attachments to natural spaces and places, then society will ultimately fail to raise the next generation of stewards who will care for and protect their environment. Furthermore, youth today have few opportunities to engage in important community issues, and as a result, many youth report feeling disengaged from their communities (Hart & Atkins, 2002; The Nature Conservancy, 2011). Nature needs youth who are prepared and educated, and children need ways to engage with their communities. Experiences in nature can address both.

Camp experiences provide one strategy for youth engagement and also promote a number of positive developmental benefits to youth (Bialeschki, Henderson, & James, 2007; Thurber et al., 2007). Camp and other informal educational experiences are well suited to exposing children to nature, helping them to develop an affinity for their natural environment and providing opportunities for them to practice service and develop greater environmental awareness and literacy.

Positive Youth Development, Leadership, and Environmental Stewardship

The positive youth development framework, upon which this book was written, assumes that youth are inherently prone toward optimal development and given the necessary support systems (i.e., supports and opportunities) will become healthy and productive adults (Lerner et al., 2005; Pittman et al., 2003). Four of the supports and opportunities necessary for positive youth development are supportive relationships, safety, skill building, and youth involvement and decision making.

A key component of youth involvement is leadership. MacNeil (2006) suggests that youth leadership is "a relational process combining ability with authority to positively influence...communities" (p. 29). Leadership has been an important dimension of the camp experience for decades, with approximately 42% of ACA-accredited and -affiliated camps currently offering leadership development programs (American Camp Association, 2011b). Camp-based leadership programs take many forms—from training programs that develop future camp counselors and staff to on- and off-site service learning programs that focus on community improvement. Leadership experiences integrated into camp involvement support the development of what have been defined as "21st century competencies." These competencies include such skills as critical thinking, problem solving, collaboration, adaptability, initiative, and environmental literacy skills—all of which have been defined as critical for youth to succeed in the modern workplace (Partnership for 21st Century Skills, 2011).

Youth often learn best when they have an opportunity to create a product or service that adds value to others. Environmental stewardship, a multifaceted concept in which a person's attitudes and beliefs about the environment compel pro-environmental action (Kals, Schumacher, & Montada, 1999), is one example of service that can be integrated into camp leadership programs. Service through youth-led environmental stewardship projects is one valuable strategy through which young people can be involved in meaningful leadership. Engaging youth in issues related to environmental stewardship is a promising route by which the positive outcomes commonly associated with youth involvement and leadership may be achieved (Browne, Garst, & Bialeschki, 2011).

Goal of This Book

The goal of this book, which is based on the ACA's national Camp 2 Grow program, is to provide youth program providers with a resource for teaching youth about leadership and environmental stewardship. Camp 2 Grow was developed by the ACA through funding from the Lilly Endowment to teach youth fundamental leadership knowledge and skills and to provide them with a framework for implementing environmental stewardship applications in their camps, homes, schools, and communities.

This book has been adapted from the Camp 2 Grow program materials and promising practices learned from implementing Camp 2 Grow. Because this book was implemented with youth from a variety of resident camps, day camps, and even after-school programs and because program evaluation results guided curriculum modifications across the three implementation years, this curriculum is viewed as a promising model for teaching youth about leadership and environmental stewardship in a variety of youth program and summer learning settings. Research on the outcomes of Camp 2 Grow indicates that the program enhanced youth skills in independence, empowerment, and problem solving. Camp 2 Grow also taught youth how to become environmental stewards and strengthened their emotional connections with nature (see the logic model and evaluation plan outlined in Chapter 12 for more information).

Book Foundations and Components

Integrated Components

This book has three integrated components: leadership training, nature-based problem-solving practice, and environmental stewardship planning. The foundation of this book includes 17 leadership lessons, integrated through Chapters 2 through 10, that focus on the core areas of leadership, character, teamwork, building relationships, taking initiative, setting goals, and solving problems (Figure 1-1). These lessons are explored through a variety of individual and group activities and exercises. Integrated into a number of these lessons are environmental applications that allow youth to practice nature-based problem solving by using a variety of scenarios. Finally, in Chapter 11, youth are guided in the completion of a specific "take home" environmental stewardship action plan, which allows them to outline how they will address an environmental problem or issue in their camps, homes, schools, and communities.

Educational Program Model for Environmental Stewardship

Different approaches exist for teaching environmental stewardship. This book is based on an educational model that takes young people from leadership awareness to environmental stewardship (Figure 1-2). The learning emphasis taught through the curriculum in this book is placed on leadership, as opposed to environmental education, with the application of leadership emphasizing nature-based problem solving. Thus, this book teaches young leaders how to use their leadership skills to address environmental problems rather than producing young naturalists.

Leadership

- Defining leadership
- Leadership styles

Character

- Understanding values, beliefs, character, and integrity
- Understanding responsibility and accountability

Teamwork

- Defining teamwork
- Roles of leaders on teams
- Importance of attitude on a team

Building Positive Relationships

- Importance of building relationships

Service

- Defining service
- Finding opportunities for service

Taking Initiative and Getting Results

- Being a self-starter

Goal Setting

- Setting goals
- Developing a plan by using a goal

Problem Solving

- Defining problem solving
- Resources available
- Developing solutions and strategies
- Identifying others to help

Figure 1-1. Leadership skills targeted

The importance of developing in youth an emotional connection to nature is recognized in the model that guides this book. Environmental stewardship behaviors often originate in an emotional connection to nature (Kals, Schumacher, & Montada, 1999). Young people may develop this emotional connection, also referred to as an affinity for nature, when they have meaningful experiences in the outdoors at a young

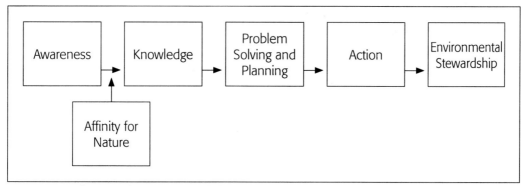

Figure 1-2. Educational program model

The learning emphasis taught through the curriculum in this book is placed on leadership, as opposed to environmental education, with the application of leadership emphasizing nature-based problem solving.

age. Meaningful outdoor experiences are often correlated to stronger environmentalism (The Nature Conservancy, 2011). Camp experiences can provide meaningful experiences in the outdoors. Resources for enhancing an affinity for nature in youth are presented in Appendix G. In addition, the sample youth surveys provided in Appendices B and C have integrated the ACA's Affinity for Nature outcome scale (Sibthorp, 2008) [one scale in the Youth Outcomes Battery (Ellis, Sibthorp, & Bialeschki, 2007)] so organizations can measure how their leadership and environmental stewardship programs might impact youths' emotional connection to nature.

This book is also based on the following principles of learning (Chan, McDermott, & Roediger, 2007; Rubinstein, Meyer, & Evans, 2001; Willis, 2008):
- Youth learn best in environments where relationships foster respect and risk taking.
- Youth learn best when they engage in experiences that elicit or build on their prior knowledge and experience.
- Youth learn best when they acquire knowledge that answers questions that are meaningful and relevant to themselves.
- Youth learn best and reach mastery when they rehearse knowledge in multiple ways.
- Youth learn best when they assess their growth and use feedback for improvement.
- Youth learn best when they create products or services that add value to others.

Chapter Characteristics

The content of Chapters 2 through 11 is summarized at the beginning of each chapter. Through these chapters, participants learn about leadership and environmental stewardship by being led through a series of activities. Chapters 2 through 11 have the following general characteristics:

- Lessons build increasing skill and mastery.
- Lessons are correlated with national education standards.
- Lessons build on one another with an intentional scope and sequence.
- Lessons include exercises, several of which involve nature-based problem solving, which require reflection, practice, and real-world application.

These chapters include the following components:

- Learning emphasis
- Time required
- Materials needed
- Activity agenda
- Chapter connection to environmental stewardship project
- Related activities and exercises
- Application and assessment opportunities

Participant Journaling

Several of the activities in this book encourage the use of a participant journal. The facilitator (i.e., the staff member using this book and guiding youth through the activities) can determine the best way to give participants time to reflect and write in their journals every day. Journaling has been found to be an impactful tool for reflection and learning among youth, and the ideas shared and explored through journaling are an important part of a successful leadership training program. The following are a few tips adapted from Bialeschki (2009) to help maximize participants' journaling experience:

- A journal is essentially a diary used for intentional reflection based on concepts being learned. Some journals included guiding questions.
- Each participant should receive his own journal that he can keep. Ask participants to write their names in their journals.
- Journaling is a tool for reflection on a particular idea. Grammar, writing style, punctuation, or other things that youth might normally pay attention to when writing are not important. Expressing thoughts and feelings are what count in journaling.
- Journals are private. If a person wants to share ideas he wrote about in the journal, that is fine, but no one should be forced to share what he wrote.
- Journaling is a great way for participants to remember how they felt about something at a particular time—even after they have been away from it for a long period of time.

Recommendations for Program Success

Based on promising practices learned from the use of the program materials in this book in the Camp 2 Grow program, the following recommendations adapted from Garst & Chavez (2010) will help you integrate this book into your leadership and environmental stewardship program:

- *Target older youth interested in leadership.* The chapter activities in this book are designed for youth ages 12 and up and are ideal for youth who are participating in a leadership development program (sometimes called a counselor in training [CIT] or leaders in training [LIT] program) and who have direct opportunities to apply new knowledge and skills they will learn through the activities in this book.

- *Proper planning is critical.* Facilitators using this book need to plan ahead by reading the applicable chapters/activities and being properly prepared. In many ways, the facilitator will act as a translator; he must strike the right balance between what is being said by the curriculum and what is going to be understood by the youth who may be used to a different way of doing or learning.

- *Be flexible with teaching spaces.* Keep in mind that many of the chapter activities can be taught in a variety of settings. You can use a standardized teaching space, such as a room, gazebo, pavilion, etc., but you can also use other spaces in and around your organization's site, including nature. For example, participants can explore setting goals while walking to the lake or have a more formal sit-down note-taking session around a fire pit. Discussions on styles of leadership can be conducted at the low ropes course in order to debrief actual demonstrations of leadership that took place in the moment. Conversations on teamwork and problem solving can be integrated into emergent teachable moments on a nature trail. Be open to these opportunities, and encourage facilitators who are teaching your leadership and environmental stewardship program to be creative.

- *Coordinate with community resources.* The program described in this book culminates with participants developing an environmental stewardship project that they will implement in their camps, homes, schools, and communities. Although participants will have a plan in hand, youth will likely need additional community support (when they return home after completing your program) to facilitate the completion of their plans.

We encourage camps and other organizations using this book to consider ways to facilitate leadership opportunities and environmental projects while participants are on-site to reinforce the learning they might apply later when they return home. Helping participants become familiar with community-based resources may facilitate the completion of environmental stewardship projects. Examples of such resources are provided in Appendix F. Other strategies may enhance participants' understanding of local community resources, such as inviting community leaders to visit your organization to meet the youth participating in the leadership and environmental stewardship program. (This is one of the activities included in Chapter 11, but in order to integrate this activity, you will need to plan ahead.) Through this strategy, youth can be introduced to community resources that might be helpful to them as they implement their projects and community leaders can learn more about the engaged young people from your organization who are interested in improving their communities by working to solve nature-based problems.

2

Leadership

Learning Emphasis
- Define leadership.
- Identify leadership opportunities available in the participant's life.
- Identify five leadership styles.
- Identifying strengths and challenges of each participant's predominant leadership style.

Time Required
- 60–90 minutes (depending on number of activities completed)

Materials Needed
- Leadership activities
- Pen/pencil for each participant
- Writing surface (poster board, flip chart) and markers
- Participant journal (optional)
- Handouts A through H

Activity Agenda
- Chapter Connection to Environmental Stewardship Project
- Leadership Island Activity
- How I Show Leadership Activity
- Identifying Leaders Activity
- Identifying Leadership Characteristics Activity
- Eyewitness News Activity
- Exploring Leadership Styles Activity
- Strengths and Weaknesses of Leadership Styles Activity
- Identifying Your Leadership Style Activity
- Exploring What We Learned Today

Chapter Connection to Environmental Stewardship Project

⇨ Facilitator Says: *"In this portion of our leadership program, we will be learning about leadership characteristics. Remember that we will all be challenged at the end of the program with leading an environmental project. Participants who understand their own leadership style and who are able to identify positive leadership qualities in others will be better able to model leadership in ways that are appropriate for a given situation, thus improving the likelihood of successful project implementation."*

Leadership Island Activity

• Distribute Handout A ("Leadership Characteristics") to each participant.

• Split the large group into smaller groups of three to five participants. Each group should imagine they are stranded on Leadership Island. This island is loaded with "leadership characteristic trees." In order for participants to get off the island and back to civilization, each group must pick five different characteristics from the trees and develop a convincing case as to why these characteristics will help them become successful in life. Because this is an opening exercise, you should be mainly concerned with each group coming up with positive reasons why its leadership characteristics will help them be successful. The answers are neither right nor wrong.

⇨ Facilitator Says: *"Imagine you and your group are stranded on Leadership Island. The only way for you to get back to civilization is to choose five leadership characteristics that you think are important to becoming successful. These characteristics can be found on the leadership trees you have in front of you. You must develop a case as to why these characteristics are important and then present your case to the Supreme Leader, which is me. If your case is convincing, I will grant you passage back to civilization, where you can create a successful future. You will have six minutes to complete this activity. Are there any questions? Go."*

• Discuss what participants came up with. Participant responses might include:
    ✓ Trustworthy is needed in order to build personal and business relationships.
    ✓ Honesty is a key component to building trust.
    ✓ Being a good listener is important for developing an understanding of others' needs.
    ✓ Humor helps people enjoy being around you.
    ✓ A willingness to cooperate and work with others can help accomplish more than someone working alone.

How I Show Leadership Activity

⇨ Facilitator Says: *"Considering the activity you just completed, what do you think of when you hear the word leadership?"*

• You may choose to share Handout B, which shows words that are often associated with leadership.

⇨ Facilitator Says: *"Now I would like you to think about how you define leadership. Take a moment to think about it and then share your definition with someone sitting next to you."*

• Share Handout C. Discuss how participants' definitions were similar to or different from the definition on Handout C, which is "Leadership is influence and the ability to obtain followers."

• Next, have participants brainstorm all the ways they are leaders based on the definition.

⇨ Facilitator Says: *"In your journals, write down how many opportunities you currently have, based on this definition, to show leadership. Your examples can include leadership at camp, at school, at home, and in your community."*

• Ask selected participants to share their examples of leadership and then record the examples on a flip chart. Some of the examples might include:
   ✓ Listen to a friend who may have a problem.
   ✓ Encourage a teammate.
   ✓ Sincerely compliment someone.
   ✓ Help a friend study for a test.
   ✓ Take charge of a committee at school.
   ✓ Volunteer to do community service.
   ✓ Pick up trash you find in the school hallway.

Identifying Leaders Activity

• Give participants Handout D and then ask them to identify two leaders in each of the categories listed on the handout. Give participants approximately five minutes to do this.

   ✓ Facilitator Says: *"Using the handout provided, identify two people you consider leaders in each of the following categories. Write their names in the spots identified on the handout. When I say 'Leaders,' you will have three minutes to select and write the names in the appropriate area. Are there any questions? 'Leaders!'"*

Identifying Leadership Characteristics Activity

- Using Handout D, have participants identify leadership characteristics of the people they selected as leaders. Give participants five to six minutes to complete this section. (You might suggest having them refer back to Handout A for a list of leadership characteristics.)

  ⇨ Facilitator Says: *"Now that you have identified your leaders, list the leadership characteristics these people have that distinguish them as leaders."*

Characteristics of Leaders from Handout A

- *Vision Characteristics:* Creative, forward thinking, enthusiastic, establishes goals, focused, intuitive, innovative, change agent

- *Relationship Characteristics:* Compassionate, motivates others, understanding, empathetic, serving, team developing, respectful, good listener, appreciative of others

- *Awareness Characteristics:* Self-awareness, global awareness, community involvement, environmental awareness, open to diversity

- *Character Characteristics:* Courageous, ethical, persevering, self-disciplined, responsible, humble, loyal, trustworthy, honest, sense of humor

- *Action Characteristics:* Risk taker, decision maker, empowering, problem solver, strong work ethic, evaluator of outcomes, effective communicator

- *Continuous Improvement:* Embraces innovation, lifelong learner, adaptability, can be coached

  ⇨ Facilitator Says: *"We have taken a look at various characteristics that are found among leaders. Let's now see if we can define what leadership is."*

Eyewitness News Activity

- Show participants a partial list of leadership characteristics using Handout A. Have participants pair up. Participants should pick at least three leadership characteristics they think are most important in a staff member/counselor/leader and then briefly tell why. They will have 60 seconds. At the end of 60 seconds, they switch roles of interviewer and interviewee.

  ⇨ Facilitator Says: *"We have talked about many leadership characteristics. You will now interview one another. One person will ask the other, 'What three leadership characteristics do you feel are most important in a staff member/counselor/ leader and why?' The person being interviewed will have 60 seconds to answer. At the end of 60 seconds, switch roles and then repeat this exercise. The interview might include such questions as:*

✓ *What is leadership?*

✓ *What kind of leadership opportunities do people experience here?*

✓ *What is the common leadership style used here? Can you give examples of that leadership style used in action?*

✓ *How do you overcome your leadership style challenges?"*

- Challenge your participants. Instruct participants that during the course of the program session—or a time span you deem appropriate—they should identify three opportunities to influence someone in a positive manner.

  ⇨ Facilitator Says: *"For the next week, you are to identify three opportunities that you have had to influence someone in a positive manner. At the end of the week, we will talk about these opportunities."*

Exploring Leadership Styles Activity

  ⇨ Facilitator Says: *"Now that we know what leadership is, what do you think leadership style means?"*

- Ask participants to think about this question, find a partner to discuss their answer with, and then share their interpretation of a leadership style. After hearing a few definitions, move on to the definitions.

  ⇨ Facilitator Says: *"Those are some excellent definitions and are very close to the one we will use today. This handout shows the definitions of leadership styles that we will use. Leadership styles are what leaders do. Leadership styles are also how leaders act according to what they value."*

- Share Handout E (definitions of leadership styles).

- Distribute Handout F "Leadership Style Inventory" and then follow the instructions in the activity.

  ⇨ Facilitator Says: *"For each section, place an X by the statement that best describes you. Try to come to a final decision on your response choice in every case. If you find this choice hard to make in one or two cases, place a check mark beside your second choice."*

- Break participants into groups according to the letter that was the most dominant for each participant.

⇨ Facilitator Says: *"Keep in mind that all the letters or styles are good, and one is not more important or better than another. That being said, let's break up into groups according to your dominant letter: As will be at the back-left of the room, Bs will be at the back-right of the room, Cs will be in the center of the room, Ds will be in the front-left corner of the room, and Es will be in the front-right corner of the room. Get into your groups now."*

- Once all participants have moved into the various groups, say:

⇨ Facilitator Says: *"Within your group, take the next three minutes to come up with four attributes of your group's leadership style and then name one famous person who you think might have that leadership style. Use the questions as a guide. Begin."*

- Walk around to the groups to ensure they are not stuck, especially if a group has very few people. Use the leadership style definitions below to help if necessary. In three minutes, see if all groups are done. If so, move on. Have each group report and then move on.

⇨ Facilitator Says: *"You have excellent insight into your leadership style even though you might not have realized it. Let's talk about the names of your leadership styles and some attributes of each."*

- Once participants have come back together from their letter groups, ask one person from each group to volunteer. Each volunteer will then read the description of his letter to the group from Handout G.

Strengths and Weaknesses of Leadership Styles Activity

⇨ Facilitator Says: *"Now that we understand what leadership styles are and what our own leadership style might be, we must realize the potential strengths and challenges of each leadership style."*

- Ask participants to go back to their letter groups to brainstorm strengths and challenges. Instruct them to come up with at least two strengths and two challenges. Circulate between groups. After ample time has passed for the participants to complete the activity, bring the groups back together and then display Handout H. Only reveal one group at a time. During the discussion, ask participants what they can do to overcome the challenges listed.

Identifying Your Leadership Style Activity

- Ask participants to look back at their Inventory (Handout F).

  ⇨ Facilitator Says: *"The paper you received has the names and attributes of each leadership style. As we review these together, place a star by your most dominant style. You can use this paper to write any notes."*

- Guide the participants through each leadership style and then give the example listed. Ask participants that had that dominant style to raise their hands before you read the description.

Identify the Five Types of Leadership Styles

A. Power

   Raise your hand if "A" is your dominant style.
   - Attributes
     - ✓ Pursuit of power
     - ✓ Seeking influence and personal prestige
     - ✓ Control, authority, ultimate goal is position
     - ✓ May measure success monetarily
   - Example: Donald Trump

B. Beauty

   Raise your hand if "B" is your dominant style.
   - Attributes
     - ✓ Seeking beauty, symmetry, and harmony
     - ✓ Style is more important than practicality.
     - ✓ Self-sufficient, individualistic
     - ✓ Must have "good" taste and appearance; elegance
   - Example: Vincent Van Gogh

C. Social

   Raise your hand if "C" is your dominant style.
   - Attributes
     - ✓ Love of fellow beings
     - ✓ Humanitarian concern for welfare of others
     - ✓ Will not act for material gain without first considering others
     - ✓ The unsympathetic nature of other types is frightening.
   - Example: Mother Teresa

D. Knowledge

Raise your hand if "D" is your dominant style.

- Attributes
  - ✓ Value truth and knowledge above all thinking
  - ✓ Learning is important; knowledge is power.
  - ✓ Value science, research, and theory
  - ✓ Detached and unemotional; frustrated at failure of others
- Example: Albert Einstein

E. Resource

Raise your hand if "E" is your dominant style.

- Attributes
  - ✓ Practicality, usefulness, efficiency, and effectiveness
  - ✓ No use for knowledge that is not usable; make grades and get graded (not here to learn)
  - ✓ May look stingy/selfish
  - ✓ Life is a struggle, and you must preserve resources.
- Example: Bill Gates

Exploring What We Learned Today

The following OPTIONS are designed (a) to provide participants with more reflection opportunities, (b) to provide facilitators with a method to assess learning, and (c) to provide additional opportunities for learning to be applied. Facilitators may choose to complete *one or more of the options* from the following list based on time available and the overall goals of your organization's leadership and environmental stewardship program.

- OPTION 1: To review the styles, ask participants questions about the attributes, definition, etc. If a participant knows the answer, he should raise the appropriate number of fingers: 1 = power; 2 = beauty; 3 = social; 4 = knowledge; 5 = resource.

  ⇨ Facilitator Says: *"We are now going to play "Name That Style." An attribute will be called out, and you must determine which style it is. To answer, hold up the correct number of fingers: 1 = power; 2 = beauty; 3 = social; 4 = knowledge; 5 = resource."*

  Read the following attributes and then have participants answer:
  - ✓ This style seeks influence. (The answer is 1 = power.)
  - ✓ This style values knowledge. (The answer is 4 = knowledge.)
  - ✓ This style is all about the love of others. (The answer is 3 = social.)

✓ This style is beautiful. (The answer is 2 = beauty.)

✓ This style is just plain practical. (The answer is 5 = resource.)

- OPTION 2: Have participants keep a journal for the duration of the program session (one week, two weeks, etc.) of the daily opportunities they have to influence the lives of others. As part of this journal, they could also write about how they felt when they influenced someone in a positive manner.

- OPTION 3: Ask participants to write a brief statement about the leadership style they have the most trouble working with. In their statement, they should identify the characteristics of their style that may conflict with characteristics of the leadership style they have trouble with.

- OPTION 4: Have participants give the Leadership Styles Inventory to three other people they know and then bring the results back to the group the next day. Have participants explain their leadership style to each person they interview.

- OPTION 5: List three opportunities you have recently had to influence someone in a positive manner. Explain what action you took with this opportunity.

Handout A: Leadership Characteristics Tree

INSTRUCTIONS: The following is a list of trees and their characteristics. They are much like fruit trees, only they produce characteristics that you can pick, like you would apples or oranges. You can pick your characteristics from one tree or several.

Relationship Tree
- Motivates others
- Compassionate
- Team developing
- Understanding
- Good listener
- Appreciative of others
- Empathetic
- Respectful
- Serving

Continuous Improvement Tree
- Adaptability
- Embraces innovation
- Coachability
- Lifelong learner

Action Tree
- Decision maker
- Evaluator of outcomes
- Effective communicator
- Risk taker
- Empowering
- Problem solver
- Strong work ethic

Character Tree
- Sense of humor
- Ethical
- Trustworthy
- Responsible
- Persevering
- Courageous
- Humility
- Loyal
- Honest
- Self-disciplined

Vision Tree
- Establishes goals
- Creative
- Intuitive
- Focused
- Forward-thinking
- Innovative
- Enthusiastic
- Change agent

Awareness Tree
- Global awareness
- Self-awareness
- Open to diversity
- Community involvement
- Environmental awareness

Handout B: Terms Associated With Leadership

Decision maker?

Takes risks?

Loyal?

Humor?

Creative?

Energetic?

Adaptable?

Responsible?

Goals?

Understanding?

Honest?

Courageous?

Confident?

Friendly?

Handout C: Definition of Leadership

"Leadership is influence and the ability to obtain followers."

—John C. Maxwell

Handout D: Who Are the Leaders

INSTRUCTIONS: Identify two leaders in each of the categories listed below and then list three characteristics that distinguish these individuals as leaders.

Local Leaders

Name: _____

Leadership characteristics:

    1. _____

    2. _____

    3. _____

Name: _____

Leadership characteristics:

    1. _____

    2. _____

    3. _____

State Leaders

Name: _____

Leadership characteristics:

    1. _____

    2. _____

    3. _____

Name: _____

Leadership characteristics:

    1. _____

    2. _____

    3. _____

National or International Leaders

Name: _____

Leadership characteristics:

    1. _____

    2. _____

    3. _____

Name: _____

Leadership characteristics:

    1. _____

    2. _____

    3. _____

Handout E: Defining Leadership Styles

- Leadership styles are what leaders do.

- Leadership styles are how leaders act according to what they value.

Handout F: Leadership Style Inventory

INSTRUCTIONS: For each section, place an X by the statement that best describes you (your first choice). Try to come to a final decision on your response choice in every case. If you find this choice hard to make in one or two cases, place a check mark (✓) beside your second choice.

Dominance

_____ I belong to several groups but attend only when something really matters to me. (c)

_____ I like to work on committees, but I do not like to be the chairperson. (d)

_____ I lose interest in groups when they go along in the same old rut and do not listen to my suggestions. (a)

_____ I consciously seek and/or obtain leadership in many of my group activities. (b)

_____ I am often selected as leader of groups without seeking it. (e)

Tact

_____ People frequently misunderstand my comments. (a)

_____ My acquaintances tell me that I am noted for handling many different situations without causing ill will. (c)

_____ People rarely resent it when I must correct what they are doing or criticize them. (d)

_____ I consciously study how to handle people tactfully. (e)

_____ Before I try to get others to accept my viewpoint, I first try to find out how they feel so I can adapt my ideas to theirs. (b)

Communication

_____ I always assume the other person will be friendly, and I take the initiative in meeting him more than halfway. (e)

_____ People tell me they come to me with problems they would not even discuss with their own families. (d)

_____ I always try to give the other person some incentive or some reason for doing what I want done. (b)

_____ When a conversation lags at a party of strangers, I try to fill in the gaps by finding a topic of general interest. (c)

_____ I have some definite ideas about the failings of younger and older generations, and I do not hesitate to express them. (a)

Maturity

_____ I want what I want when I want it, regardless of consequences to others and myself. (a)

_____ I frequently let others have the last word. (e)

_____ I have been told that I can take well-meant, constructive criticism graciously. (d)

_____ I believe in telling others the truth if it is for their own good. (b)

_____ I take a stand on issues I believe in, even if they are unpopular, after looking into the pros and cons. (c)

(cont.)

Handout F: Leadership Style Inventory (cont.)

Attitudes

_____ I get annoyed when people do not do things my way. Sometimes, my temper gets the best of me. (a)

_____ I try to show the attitude toward the other person that I want them to show to me. (b)

_____ I believe I should make every effort to accept change, and I try to keep changing with the times. (e)

_____ I patiently listen to people with whom I disagree. (d)

_____ I change my mind when it comes to making a decision. Sometimes, I wait so long that circumstances force me to make a decision. (c)

Cooperation

_____ When people have a misunderstanding, I try to intervene and reconcile them. (d)

_____ In dealing with coworkers or peers, I try to put myself in their shoes and act toward them the way I would like them to act toward me. (c)

_____ I am willing to accept the help of others, provided it does not interfere with their work. (e)

_____ When I want information from others, I feel I have a right to demand it because I am acting on behalf of my boss. (a)

_____ If my boss says to me "Tell so-and-so I want this right away," I change the message and voice tone to "The boss would appreciate this as soon as possible." (b)

Calculating Your Score:

Add up Xs and checks you marked.

	First choice (X)	Second choice (✓)
TOTAL		
No. of As	_____	_____
No. of Bs	_____	_____
No. of Cs	_____	_____
No. of Ds	_____	_____
No. of Es	_____	_____

Identify Your Leadership Style (from the total number of Xs and ✓s.)

_____ This is your predominant style.   _____ You have tendencies in this direction.

Handout G:
Identifying Types of Leadership Styles

A. Power Style
- Attributes:
  - ✓ Pursuit of power
  - ✓ Seeking influence and personal prestige
  - ✓ Control, authority, ultimate goal is position
  - ✓ May measure success monetarily
- Example: Donald Trump

B. Beauty Style
- Attributes:
  - ✓ Seeking beauty, symmetry, and harmony
  - ✓ Style is more important than practicality.
  - ✓ Self-sufficient, individualistic
  - ✓ Must have "good" taste and appearance; elegance
- Example: Vincent Van Gogh

C. Social Style
- Attributes:
  - ✓ Love of fellow beings
  - ✓ Humanitarian concern for welfare of others
  - ✓ Will not act for material gain without first considering others
  - ✓ The unsympathetic nature of other types is frightening.
- Example: Mother Teresa

D. Knowledge Style
- Attributes:
  - ✓ Value truth and knowledge above all thinking
  - ✓ Learning is important; knowledge is power.
  - ✓ Value science, research, and theory
  - ✓ Detached and unemotional; frustrated at failure of others
- Example: Albert Einstein

E. Resource Style
- Attributes:
  - ✓ Practicality, usefulness, efficiency, and effectiveness
  - ✓ No use for knowledge that is not usable; make grades and get graded (not here to learn)
  - ✓ May look stingy/selfish
  - ✓ Life is a struggle, and you must preserve resources.
- Example: Bill Gates

Handout H:
Strengths and Challenges of
Each Leadership Style

A. Power

- Strengths: clearly sees goals; respects authority

- Challenges: does not always consider others' feelings; does not always take into consideration the consequences of certain decisions

B. Beauty

- Strengths: truly appreciates beautiful things in life; can take care of themselves

- Challenges: does not always seek the input of others; reputation means too much

C. Social

- Strengths: truly cares for others and their welfare; always thinks about others' needs

- Challenges: does not make decisions for themselves; can be offended easily when someone else is not being sympathetic

D. Knowledge

- Strengths: good thinkers; can make a decision without becoming emotionally attached

- Challenges: frustrated by others, especially if underachieving; does not think of others when making a decision

E. Resource

- Strengths: has a lot of common sense; saves money

- Challenges: can be considered stingy/selfish; hard time seeing the purpose in knowledge or social interactions

3

Character

Learning Emphasis
- Define values, beliefs, character, and integrity.
- Relate values, beliefs, character, and integrity to leaders' daily choices.
- Understand the importance of being personally responsibility and accountable for your actions as a leader.

Time Required
- 60–90 minutes (depending on number of activities completed)

Materials Needed
- Character activities
- Pen/pencil for each participant
- Writing surface (poster board, flip chart) and markers
- Mirror
- Scenario cards
- Participant journal (optional)
- Handouts I through M

Activity Agenda
- Chapter Connection to Environmental Stewardship Project
- Mirror Activity
- Qualities of Character Activity
- Create-a-Skit Activity
- Scenario Cards Activity
- Being a Responsible and Accountable Leader Activity
- Exploring What We Learned Today

Chapter Connection to Environmental Stewardship Project

⇨ Facilitator Says: *"In this portion of our leadership program, we will be learning about character. Remember that we will all be challenged at the end of the program with leading an environmental project. Participants who understand their values, beliefs, character, integrity, responsibility, and accountability will be better prepared and able to demonstrate the qualities of a leader. Participants will be more likely to successfully lead others because of their demonstrated character and willingness to take responsibility and be accountable, thus improving the likelihood of project implementation."*

Mirror Activity

- Walk around the room and hold a mirror in front of each person's face.

    ⇨ Facilitator Says: *"What do you see?"*

- Elicit answers.

    ⇨ Facilitator Says: *"Today, we are going to dig deep, peel back some layers, and reflect on the images we just saw in the mirror. To do this, we need to practice openness, honesty, and respect for ourselves and peers."*

    ⇨ Facilitator Says: *"Let's get started. Think of five things that are important to you in your life. You have 30 seconds to write them down. Prioritize them from most important to least important. Begin now."*

- While participants are reflecting, pass out sheets of poster paper and markers for participants to capture their thoughts.

    ⇨ Facilitator Says: *"Now draw a series of three pictures on this sheet of poster paper. Each picture should symbolize the three most important things in your life. The size of the picture is relative to its importance. Thus, the most important things in your life should be bigger than the less important things in your life. Take five minutes to work on your pictures."*

- After five minutes, ask participants to take a moment to share their top three with the person next to them and then proceed.

    ⇨ Facilitator Says: *"Take a moment to share your drawing with the person next to you."*

- Have participants tape their posters around the room. When participants are finished, ask for three volunteers to discuss their drawings with the rest of the group. After each of the three participants have shared, make the following comment:

  ⇨ Facilitator Says: *"Now focus on your largest picture. Explain why you chose that one."*

- Let each participant share.

Qualities of Character Activity

⇨ Facilitator Says: *"Just as each of us is unique on the outside, we are also unique on the inside. Look at the posters we created and see how everyone values things differently. People define things differently because of their own experiences."*

- Share Handout I, which provides definitions for values, beliefs, character, and integrity. Examples are provided in the activity to help establish definitions.
  - ✓ Values: "Things we believe in strongly. Things we do not compromise or change." Examples: health, family, and service to others. Values are shaped at an early age. Parents, facilitators, friends, religious leaders, and heroes help shape our values. Three tests of a value are that they must be freely chosen, cherished, and acted on.
  - ✓ Beliefs: "The conviction that something is right." Examples: telling the truth, faith. I may believe in something but not freely choose it, cherish it, or act on it.
  - ✓ Character: "Common attitudes, beliefs, and behaviors valued by society for people to demonstrate as responsible citizens." Examples: work ethic, punctuality, and willingness to take constructive criticism. Common categories of character may include: Trustworthiness, Respect, Responsibility, Fairness, Caring, and Citizenship. Character traits are usually determined by the society where we live.
  - ✓ Integrity: "When what a person says and what they do are in alignment." Example: ethics, morals. Integrity does not change when we are around different people.

  ⇨ Facilitator says: *"Think about a leader you know (teacher, friend, staff member, counselor, mentor, etc.) who you think shows values, beliefs, character, or integrity. Write down statements of values, beliefs, character, and integrity that the person shows. Go."*

- Participants complete the exercise.

  ⇨ Facilitator says: *"Great job, everybody. Now choose two partners to share what you wrote about the leader you know and how that person shows values, beliefs, character, and integrity. Take five minutes for this activity."*

⇨ Facilitator Says: *"Based on our brainstorming activity on leaders and their characteristics, we now know that attributes drive a person's life. But how many of us realize the impact on our lives of values, beliefs, character, and integrity?"*

Create-a-Skit Activity

⇨ Facilitator Says: *"The following activity will help us see how values, beliefs, character, and integrity can help us as future leaders in our community."*

• Arrange participants into four groups. Each group will be assigned one of the four topics: Values, Beliefs, Character, or Integrity. Instruct participants to create a one-minute skit within their group to act out how their assigned topic can help them as future leaders. After ample time has passed for groups to prepare, each team will perform for the group. Group 1 will brainstorm about values; Group 2, beliefs; Group 3, character; and Group 4, integrity.

• Write down two to three ideas from each group as they perform their skits. Share the following. (You can use Handout J as a guide for participants.)

⇨ Facilitator Says: *"How do values, beliefs, character, and integrity benefit leaders? The following are some ways. Select at least three and then add them to your personal list. Values, beliefs, character, and integrity help provide:*
   ✓ *Credibility*
   ✓ *Decision-making skills*
   ✓ *Direction*
   ✓ *Emotional stability*
   ✓ *Healthy lifestyle*
   ✓ *Lasting positive reputation*
   ✓ *Positive attitude*
   ✓ *Self-discipline*
   ✓ *Self-esteem*
   ✓ *Structure"*

⇨ Facilitator Says: *"Now let's look at how the choices we make are based on the values, beliefs, character, and integrity we have. Let's not think only as leaders, now and in the future, but also in each little daily choice that we make. We are now going to peel a little deeper and think inwardly about actually being faced with a decision regarding what we are going to do based on our set of values, beliefs, character, and integrity."*

Scenario Cards Activity

⇨ Facilitator Says: *"Now let's talk about how values, beliefs, character, and integrity affect our daily choices. Each of you will receive a scenario card to read. When I say 'Share,' turn to a peer and then read your scenario. Ask him for his answer to the question on the scenario card. Share your answer with one another to see if you agree."*

• Hand scenario cards to two participants working as a team. Make sure that each team receives a different scenario. Show Handout K.

⇨ Facilitator Says: *"Ready? Read your scenarios."*

• When participants are finished, share additional examples of how values, beliefs, character, and integrity affect leaders' daily choices.

⇨ Facilitator Says: *"How do values, beliefs, character, and integrity impact our daily choices? The following are some ways. Values, beliefs, character, and integrity impact…*
✓ *The food we eat.*
✓ *The exercise we do or do not do.*
✓ *The way we treat parents, siblings, friends, and others.*
✓ *The clothes we wear.*
✓ *The way we drive to work or school.*
✓ *The stories we tell or do not tell.*
✓ *The compassion we show to those in need."*

• After each group has had time to talk about its scenario, ask for a volunteer from each group. Volunteers will then come to the front to share about their scenario and discussion. After each volunteer shares, ask "Who would have done it differently and why?"

• Conclude this part of the activity by reminding participants that our values, beliefs, character, and integrity affect everything we do each day and every decision we make no matter how big or small.

Being a Responsible and Accountable Leader Activity

• Brainstorm a list of words or phrases that describe a responsible and accountable person. Compare the list developed by participants with the list from Handout L. (Take about 10 minutes.)

⇨ Facilitator Says: *"As a group, let's think of as many words or phrases that might help us describe responsibility and accountability. Raise your hand when you think of a word and we will place it on the writing surface. Be thoughtful and courteous to yourself and others as they are quietly thinking and writing down their responses. Let's begin."*

- Examples might include:
    - ✓ Job
    - ✓ Duty
    - ✓ Completing a task
    - ✓ Dependability
    - ✓ Liability
    - ✓ Answerability
    - ✓ Being reliable
    - ✓ Doing what you say you will do
    - ✓ Not blaming others
    - ✓ Fulfilling obligations
    - ✓ Making good judgments
    - ✓ Exercising self-control

- Read the following definition and then ask participants to answer the following questions.

    ⇨ Facilitator Says: *"One definition of being responsible and accountable is 'To be regularly answerable for key areas of our lives with qualified people.'"*

- If you are using a flip chart, underline the key words "regularly," "answerable," "key areas," and "qualified" as you ask them the four questions.

    ⇨ Facilitator Says:
    - ✓ *"What does 'regularly' mean?*
    - ✓ *What does 'answerable' mean?*
    - ✓ *What are some examples of key areas that might apply to a staff member/ counselor/leader that works here?*
    - ✓ *Can you think of a time when you have been accountable?"*

- Discuss with participants the positive and negative consequences of their actions with the following activity. Divide the group into smaller groups of three. Have each small group create a list of five "dos" and "don'ts" for being responsible and accountable. After ample time has passed, ask for a volunteer to share. While participants are sharing, the facilitator should make these lists visible to the entire group to see.

    ⇨ Facilitator Says: *"Let's continue keeping our creative juices flowing and create a list of the "dos" and "don'ts" for being responsible and accountable."*

- Once all smaller groups have shared, ask participants:

  ⇨ Facilitator Says: *"Is there anything that belongs on the 'dos' and 'don'ts' list that we have not discussed?"*

- Discuss the following questions with your participants:
  - ✓ What happens when leaders show the behaviors in the "dos" list?
  - ✓ What happens when leaders show the behaviors in the "don'ts" list?
  - ✓ In what ways does irresponsible behavior affect our community here? Our home community? Our school community?
  - ✓ How can young leaders today (like us) demonstrate personal responsibility and accountability?

Exploring What We Learned Today

The following OPTIONS are designed (a) to provide participants with more reflection opportunities, (b) to provide facilitators with a method to assess learning, and (c) to provide additional opportunities for learning to be applied. Facilitators may choose to complete *one or more of the options* from the following list based on time available and the overall goals of your organization's leadership and environmental stewardship program.

  ⇨ Facilitator Says: *"Today, we started our exploration of character by looking at ourselves in the mirror. Is the person we see in the mirror truly us? (The reply from participants should be "No.") Each of us is defined by our 'character.' We have to look deeper to understand our character—to see who each of us really is. Who we really are on the inside shows by what we do and say on the outside. Each of us today peeled back layers of ourselves and began to understand more about our values, beliefs, character, and integrity and how we show these qualities in our lives and around others. We also learned what it means to be responsible and accountable, which is particularly important when we are serving in leadership roles at camp, at home, at school, and in our communities."*

- OPTION 1: Ask participants to think back in history and then write down the name of a famous historical figure and identify values, beliefs, character, and integrity that person exhibited.

- OPTION 2: Discuss the following questions and answers.
  - ✓ What are the three tests for something to be considered a value?
    - Values are shaped at an early age.
    - Parents, facilitators, friends, religious leaders, and heroes help shape our values.
    - Three tests for a value are: It must be freely chosen, must be cherished, and must be acted on.

✓ What are five ways values, beliefs, character, and integrity can impact our daily lives? Answers should include five of the following:
  - The amount of sleep we get each day
  - The food we eat
  - The exercise we do or do not do
  - The way we treat parents, siblings, friends, and others
  - The clothes we wear
  - The way we drive to work or school
  - The way we choose to greet each other
  - The answers we give to questions asked of us
  - The stories we tell or do not tell
  - The service we provide to our community
  - The compassion we show to those in need
  - The amount of studying we do
  - The tips we give to those who serve us
  - The energy we put into our jobs
  - The quality we put into everything we do
  - The decisions we make

✓ Which of the following statements are "true" and which are "false"?
  - We begin to form our values in our teen years. (False)
  - Respect is a common category describing character. (True)
  - Our integrity changes as we meet different people. (False)
  - Character traits are rarely determined by the society we live in. (False)
  - Beliefs and values are different. (True)

- OPTION 3: Many leaders in our communities can provide a greater insight about values, beliefs, character, and integrity. Have participants identify a (counselor, member of the staff, other) and then conduct a personal interview about how the leader's values, beliefs, character, and integrity are important for being a good leader. (You can use Handout M as a guide for participants.)

- OPTION 4: Ask participants to make a list of the ways that they demonstrate responsibility and accountability here and at school.

- OPTION 5: Have participants sketch in their journals about being responsible and accountable. After participants are finished, instruct them to find a partner to share their sketches with. Finish the activity by asking for a few volunteers to share their sketches with the group.

Handout I:
Defining Values, Beliefs, Character, and Integrity

Values

Values are things we believe in strongly—things we do not compromise or change.

- ✓ Values are shaped at an early age.
- ✓ Parents, teachers, friends, religious leaders, and heroes help shape our values.
- ✓ Three tests for a value are: It must be freely chosen, cherished, and acted on.

Beliefs

A belief is the conviction that something is right. I may believe in something but not freely choose it, cherish it, or act on it.

Character

Character can be described as the common attitudes, beliefs, and behaviors valued by society for people to demonstrate as responsible citizens. Character traits usually are determined by the society we live in. Common categories of character may include:

- ✓ Trustworthiness
- ✓ Respect
- ✓ Responsibility
- ✓ Fairness
- ✓ Caring
- ✓ Citizenship

Integrity

- ✓ Integrity is when what a person says and what he does are in alignment.
- ✓ Integrity does not change when we are around different people

Handout J:
How Values, Beliefs, Character, and Integrity Benefit Leaders

Values, beliefs, character, and integrity help provide:

✓ Credibility

✓ Decision making

✓ Direction

✓ Emotional stability

✓ Lasting positive reputation

✓ Positive attitude

✓ Self-discipline

✓ Self-esteem

✓ Structure

Handout K:
Scenarios for
"Scenario Cards Activity"

- *Scenario #1:* During an afternoon activity, you are warned by a teacher for "talking while someone else was talking." You believe you were not talking out of turn but was answering a question that another person had asked you about the activity. How would your values, beliefs, character, and integrity shape the way you handle the situation?

- *Scenario #2:* It is the first day of camp. You are in your cabin/lodge organizing your things when another teen who is assigned to your cabin/lodge walks in. He is dressed differently from you and the other teens in your cabin. One of the other teens begins to ridicule the teen after his parents leave. How would your values, beliefs, character, and integrity shape the way you handle the situation?

- *Scenario #3:* A "Teen of the Year Award" is given to one teen in every cabin each year at the end of the program. To earn it, you must keep track of the points you earn for competing different activities. Your counselor wants you to win this award, and he suggests you log extra points that you did not actually earn. How would your values, beliefs, character, and integrity shape the way you handle the situation?

- *Scenario #4:* You promised a camp friend that you would sit with him on the last night of camp at dinner. Then, one of your other camp friends asks you to sit at his table, which has only one seat left. How would your values, beliefs, character, and integrity shape the way you handle the situation?

Handout L:
Examples of Responsibility
and Accountability

✓ Job

✓ Duty

✓ Completing a task

✓ Dependability

✓ Liability

✓ Answerability

✓ Being reliable

✓ Doing what you say you will do

✓ Not blaming others

✓ Fulfilling obligations

✓ Making good judgments

✓ Exercising self-control

Handout M: Participant Interview Guide: Values, Beliefs, Character, and Integrity

INSTRUCTIONS: Prepare two questions for each of the following key terms to ask someone you respect and who demonstrates your understanding of today's activity.

Interviewer: _____

Interviewee: _____

Values

• Question 1:

　✓ Respondent's answer:

• Question 2:

　✓ Respondent's answer:

Beliefs

• Question 1:

　✓ Respondent's answer:

• Question 2:

　✓ Respondent's answer:

Character

• Question 1:

　✓ Respondent's answer:

• Question 2:

　✓ Respondent's answer:

Integrity

• Question 1:

　✓ Respondent's answer:

• Question 2:

　✓ Respondent's answer:

4

Teamwork

Learning Emphasis
- Differentiate between a group and a team.
- Identify leader roles within a team.
- Define teamwork and identify six benefits to working in teams.
- List qualities a leader should look for in others when putting together a team.
- Assess personal ability to exhibit different leadership roles.

Time Required
- 60–90 minutes (depending on number of activities completed)

Materials Needed
- Teamwork activities
- Pen/pencil for each participant
- Writing surface (poster board, flip chart) and markers
- Materials used in baking (rolling pin, large spoons, whisk, mixing bowl, apron)
- Soft foam ball
- One cookie for each participant (optional)
- Participant journal (optional)
- Handouts N through T

Activity Agenda
- Chapter Connection to Environmental Stewardship Project
- Our Organizational Groups Activity
- Groups Versus Teams Activity
- Thinking About Teamwork Activity
- Teamwork Hieroglyphics Activity
- Awesome Cookie Activity
- Recycling Team Activity
- My Leadership Assessment Activity
- Exploring What We Learned Today

Chapter Connection to Environmental Stewardship Project

⇨ Facilitator Says: *"In this portion of our leadership program, we will be learning about teamwork. Remember that we will all be challenged at the end of the program with leading an environmental project. All teams need a leader, and leadership is often founded on the cooperation and involvement of others. Participants who understand teamwork dynamics and the leadership roles that are common within teams will be better able to develop a successful team based on the roles needed to complete their project, thus improving the likelihood of project implementation."*

Our Organizational Groups Activity

⇨ Facilitator Says: *"Today, we will be learning about teams and teamwork. But first, let's think about groups in general—the groups that each of us belongs to."*

- Distribute Handout N, but keep it facedown in front of each participant until you have given directions.

⇨ Facilitator Says: *"When I say 'Go,' turn over your paper and list groups—based on groups that you know of here—that begin with the different letters provided on the front of this sheet. Your goal is to think of one example for each of the letters provided. For example, if you see the letter 'C,' you may write 'Cabin Group' and 'S' might be 'Swim Class.' Any questions about this activity? Ready, set, go!"*

- Allow participants about five minutes to complete the activity. You will need a soft foam ball to toss to participants during this next activity. Elicit responses for each letter from a variety of participants. The ball is used to facilitate who is speaking. To keep the event moving, participants toss the ball to each other and then share one of their ideas.

⇨ Facilitator Says: *"Let's share our ideas. When the ball comes to you, share the example you wrote down for that letter. Then choose a person who has not shared and pass them the ball."*

- Toss the ball to a participant to begin.

⇨ Facilitator Says: *"You have created an extensive list of groups. Groups of people come in many different sizes and wear many different titles, from A to Z. How many of the groups you have on your list do you consider to be teams? Look at your list and then place a star next to those groups that you consider to be a 'team.'"*

- Facilitate responses to the question.

  ⇨ Facilitator Says: *"What criteria did you use to determine which groups are considered teams? On the side of your activity sheet, jot down a list of the criteria you used."*

- Facilitate responses to the question.

  ⇨ Facilitator Says: *"Are teams different from groups of people?"*

- Elicit responses to the question.

  ⇨ Facilitator Says: *"Other people have thought about these same questions. While both teams and groups involve a small number of people that are organized together for a specific reason, key differences exist between groups and teams. Let's take a look at those differences."*

Groups Versus Teams Activity

- Ask participants how they would define a group and then how they would define a team. You can have them work in pairs first or ask the entire group for answers.

  ⇨ Facilitator Says: *"A group is a small number of people working on the same thing. Performance comes from what members do individually."*

  ⇨ Facilitator Says: *"The following are some common characteristics of a group:*
    ✓ *A group is common and effective in large organizations where individual accountability is important.*
    ✓ *Members come together to share information and perspectives and make decisions so each person can do his job better.*
    ✓ *Members only take responsibility for themselves and no one else in the group.*
    ✓ *Groups do not become a team just because that is what someone calls them.*
    ✓ *Purpose comes from outside the group—usually top-down.*
    ✓ *Meetings run efficiently.*
    ✓ *The leader is strong and clearly focused."*

  ⇨ Facilitator Says: *"A team is a small number of people whose skills complement each other and who have committed to work together toward a common goal or goals. Performance is different with a team. With a team, the members are more interested in the performance of everyone working together because the team wants to be successful in reaching its common goal. For example, a basketball team might share a goal to reach the playoffs or a rock band might share a goal of recording a hit song."*

  ⇨ Facilitator Says: *"The following are some common characteristics of a team:*
    ✓ *A team involves individual and team accountability.*

> ✓ *Members know their performance will affect their teammates.*
> ✓ *Members hold each other accountable; they do not rely on external pressure.*
> ✓ *The team has a common purpose.*
> ✓ *Members believe in the team's purpose.*
> ✓ *Members buy into the team's purpose; it is not forced on them.*
> ✓ *Goals are derived from the team's purpose.*
> ✓ *Specific, measurable goals are best.*
> ✓ *Leadership roles are shared."*

- Ask participants to revisit the descriptions provided on Handout O and then label each description as a "team" or "group." You may also choose to share Handout P, which compares groups and teams.

  ⇨ Facilitator Says: *"Excellent work! Let's take this information to the next level. Think of a situation where working as a group would be the best way to get work done. When you have got an example, let me know by showing one thumb up."*

- Allow time to think. Gauge the amount of time based on the number of thumbs shown. Elicit responses from participants.

  ⇨ Facilitator Says: *"Excellent examples! You have it exactly right. Sometimes, working as a group will be the best way to get the work done. Other times, working as a team will be the best way to get work done. Let's dig deeper into the concept of working as a team."*

Thinking About Teamwork Activity

- If you have access to the video/DVD for *Hoosiers*, then you can choose to include this activity. Cue the part in *Hoosiers* where the state championship game starts. This clip lasts 10 minutes. Before showing the clip, share the following with participants.

  ⇨ Facilitator Says: *"It is game time! During the next few moments, you are going to get to share in an incredible moment with some individuals from Indiana. Picture this: It is the late 1950s in the small town of Hickory, Indiana. A new basketball coach has arrived at the school, and the team has undisciplined players. Let's take a look at the results of the growing pains of becoming an effective team. Put yourselves in their shoes as they face a large school opponent in the state championship game. As you watch the clip, prepare to share with the group the answer to the following question: How would you define teamwork?"*

- Play the clip.

  ⇨ Facilitator Says: *"How did you define teamwork based on the clip?"*

- Capture participants' answers on a flip chart. Share the definition of teamwork and then have participants capture it in their notes.

⇨ Facilitator Says: *"The word teamwork refers to a group of people working cooperatively to accomplish a goal. How does this definition compare and contrast with the definitions you created?"*

- Elicit responses. Continue the discussion.

⇨ Facilitator Says: *"What benefits do you see in working as a team?"*

- Elicit responses.

⇨ Facilitator Says: *"Let's take a look at some of the key benefits to teamwork* (Handout Q). *The word teamwork refers to a group of people working cooperatively to accomplish a goal. Teamwork is useful in a number of ways. Teamwork…*
  - ✓ *Fosters a sense of togetherness.*
  - ✓ *Heightens productivity.*
  - ✓ *Taps into a diversity of talents.*
  - ✓ *Shares the workload.*
  - ✓ *Balances roles of different team members (each person contributes different strengths).*
  - ✓ *Encourages risk taking."*

Teamwork Hieroglyphics Activity

- Ask participants to create a hieroglyphic (picture, icon, or image) to summarize the meaning of the term teamwork and then describe three benefits of teamwork that are most important to them.

⇨ Facilitator Says: *"Share your pictures with a person in our group who you do not know very well."*

- Allow time for participants to share.

Awesome Cookie Activity

- This activity encourages participants to think about the ingredients to make the participants better leaders in teams. Dress up like a baker and begin the discussion by holding up a rolling pin, baking tools, and a recipe card or recipe magazine as props to get the participants thinking about baking and making cookies the old-fashioned way—with hard work and the correct ingredients.

⇨ Facilitator Says: *"Does anyone know what these are?"*

- Elicit responses.

⇨ Facilitator Says: *"Have any of you used these before?"*

- Elicit responses.

  ⇨ Facilitator Says: *"What are some of the items you can make with these?"*

- Elicit responses.

  ⇨ Facilitator Says: *"How many of you have helped someone make cookies or a cake by using these materials?"*

- Elicit responses.

  ⇨ Facilitator Says: *"If you used a rolling pin, you made cookies the old-fashioned way—by adding the desired ingredients and rolling out the dough. Being a leader on teams you are a part of is like making cookies the old-fashioned way; it takes a lot of hard work and the right ingredients. Let's take a look at the ingredients for leadership on your teams and the recipes to make those ingredients work together."*

- Share Handout R.

  ⇨ Facilitator Says: *"When you are a leader of a team, you might play several different roles. Each role is different, but each is important for the success of the team. These roles include:*
    ✓ *Listener—willing to listen and not always talk*
    ✓ *Motivator—able to be the catalyst and get the team going*
    ✓ *Chemist—builds chemistry, harmony, and trust in the team*
    ✓ *Educator—provides information and strives to build themselves and team members*
    ✓ *Responsibility taker—willing to shoulder responsibility for the team*
    ✓ *Facilitator—opens up communication lines between team members*
    ✓ *Vision creator—helps develop and guide the team toward its common purpose*
    ✓ *Chef—finds the best people and assembles the best team possible."*

- Participants will draw a diagram that looks like a chocolate chip cookie as they discuss the different leader roles. The cookie will represent a team, and each "chocolate chip" will represent a role a leader must play to make that team effective. The participants will attempt to come up with the "chocolate chips." (If you are using journals, then each participant can draw his cookie in his journal. You can also do this activity in small groups by using poster board or even outside in the dirt or sand.)

  ⇨ Facilitator Says: *"It is time to be the baker. You are a skilled builder of cookies. One of the most common cookies is a chocolate chip cookie. Draw a large cookie and then draw chocolate chips about the size of a quarter on your cookies. On each chip, write a role you think a leader must play in order to make his team successful."*

- Give participants time to develop their cookies and then have them share their ideas. (You might also use this opportunity to provide a cookie or another healthy snack to each participant as a treat.)

  ⇨ Facilitator Says: *"Cookies are best when shared with other people. So, you have one minute to share your cookie with two of your neighbors. Begin sharing."*

- Have them come up with several roles that a leader must play on a team. Have them take down the following examples in their notes; if they have others that they feel are important, they should add them to the list.

  ⇨ Facilitator Says: *"Now that we know what leadership roles or ingredients we need to bake up an awesome team, let's mix in some information about what to look for to make these roles happen on a team."*

Recycling Team Activity

⇨ Facilitator Says: *"The only way to be a great baker is to assemble the best recipes. Similarly, leaders must assemble the best team of individuals possible. When this happens, the leader and the team can work toward its potential. Think about being on a team here in this program. What qualities would you want to see in the people around you to make the team successful?"*

- Elicit responses. (You may choose to use Handout S.)

  ⇨ Facilitator Says: *"Qualities that a leader should look for in others might include:*
  ✓ *Loyalty—respecting the people you work with and the team goals*
  ✓ *Good character—having a desirable set of beliefs and values*
  ✓ *Ambition—desire to work with the team*
  ✓ *Dependability—ability to be trusted with responsibilities*
  ✓ *Hardworking—willing and able to complete a job at a quality level*
  ✓ *Good attitude—focusing toward the team's success*
  ✓ *Goal oriented—putting forward resources to accomplish the team's purpose*
  ✓ *Open minded—willing to take in new ideas and work with people*
  ✓ *Knowledge, skills, and talents—they have natural abilities that complement the job; they have also practiced the skills necessary to perform on the team, and they have the knowledge necessary to be a part of the team."*

- Next, participants will be asked to think of three people they would invite to be a part of a team because they possess those qualities.

  ⇨ Facilitator Says: *"Now that you know what qualities to look for when selecting team members for specific teams, let's put that information to use. Let's say you are starting a recycling project here. Choose three people to be on your Recycling Management Team by using these qualities as a guide."*

• Discuss participants' responses.

My Leadership Assessment Activity

• Have participants assess how successful they think they are in leadership roles. Help them come up with some ideas on how to better themselves in a leadership role. Use Handout T to facilitate an assessment.

⇨ Facilitator Says: *"Good bakers are always trying to improve their recipes to make them better. This takes hard work and evaluating their success. In a moment, you will have the chance to evaluate your ability as a leader and see if you can make it better. Handout T (My Leadership Assessment) will help you evaluate yourself as a leader and help you improve in the many roles that a leader faces. What questions do you have?"*

• Next, ask participants to do the following.

⇨ Facilitator Says: *"Now do two things. First, write the two areas you scored the lowest in and then list two ways you could become better at the areas you picked."*

Exploring What We Learned Today

The following OPTIONS are designed (a) to provide participants with more reflection opportunities, (b) to provide facilitators with a method to assess learning, and (c) to provide additional opportunities for learning to be applied. Facilitators may choose to complete *one or more of the options* from the following list based on time available and the overall goals of your organization's leadership and environmental stewardship program.

• OPTION 1: Process the teamwork chapter by using the following questions: What did you learn about yourself? How will that information help you? How can you use what you learned today to create better teams?

• OPTION 2: Have participants observe a group at your site for one day. They should write down the name and description of this group and then suggest changes this group could take to become more of a team.

• OPTION 3: Have participants interview the executive director, program director, or similar leader to identify what strategies he uses to create effective work teams.

• OPTION 4: Ask participants to draw a flowchart in their journals of what they learned today about the differences between groups and teams, how a leader fits into a team, and what qualities a leader should look for when putting a team together. How does the information fit together? How can these concepts be connected? What pieces do not fit together?

Handout N: Our Organizational Groups

INSTRUCTIONS: List the groups that you know of (here in this program) that begin with the different letters provided on this sheet. Your challenge is to think of one example for each of the letters provided. For example, if you see the letter "C," you may write "Cabin Group" and "S" might be "Swim Class."

A _____

B _____

C _____

D _____

E _____

F _____

G _____

H _____

I _____

J _____

K _____

L _____

M _____

N _____

O _____

P _____

Q _____

R _____

S _____

T _____

U _____

V _____

W _____

X _____

Y _____

Z _____

Handout O: Groups vs. Teams

INSTRUCTIONS: Identify each description as either a "group" or a "team."

_____ Small number of people whose skills complement each other and who share parameters of how they will equally commit to work together.

_____ Meetings run efficiently and quickly.

_____ Performance comes from what members do individually.

_____ Performance includes results from individuals and two or more individuals working together.

_____ Small number of people working on the same thing.

_____ Often have open-ended meetings.

_____ A _____'s performance is better than the sum of all the individual bests.

_____ Individual and team accountability.

_____ Members know their performance will affect their teammates.

_____ Members hold each other accountable and do not rely on external pressure.

_____ Leader is strong and clearly focused.

_____ Members buy into common purpose; it is not forced on them.

_____ Common and effective in large organizations where individual accountability is important.

_____ Specific, measurable goals are derived from their purpose.

_____ Leadership roles are shared.

_____ Members take responsibility only for themselves and no one else in the group.

_____ Purpose comes from outside the group—usually top-down.

Handout P:
How to Tell the Difference
Between a Group and a Team

GROUP	TEAM
Strong leader	Shared leadership
Individual accountability	Individual and shared accountability
Purpose is the same as the organization's	Specific team purpose
Individual work	Collective work
Meetings are quick and efficient	Meetings are often open ended

Handout Q:
Benefits of Teamwork

- Fosters a sense of togetherness

- Heightens productivity

- Taps into a diversity of talents

- Shares the workload

- Balances roles of different team members
  (each person contributes different strengths)

- Encourages risk taking

Handout R:
Leader Roles
in a Team Activity

- Listener—willing to listen and not always talk

- Motivator—able to be the catalyst and get the team going

- Chemist—builds chemistry, harmony, and trust in the team

- Educator—provides information and strives to build himself and team members

- Responsibility taker—willing to shoulder responsibility for the team

- Facilitator—opens up communication lines between team members

- Vision creator—helps develop and guide the team toward its common purpose

- Chef—finds the best people and assembles the best team possible

Handout S:
Qualities a Leader Should
Look for in Team Members

- Loyalty—respecting the people you work with and the team goals

- Good character—having a desirable set of beliefs and values

- Ambition—desire to work with the team

- Dependability—ability to be trusted with responsibility

- Hardworking—willing and able to complete a job at a quality level

- Good attitude—focusing toward the team's success

- Goal oriented—putting forward resources to accomplish the team's purpose

- Open minded—willing to take in new ideas and work with people

- Knowledge, skills, and talents—they have natural abilities that complement the job; they have also practiced the skills necessary to perform on the team, and they have the knowledge necessary to be a part of the team

Handout T:
My Leadership Assessment

INSTRUCTIONS: Evaluate how successful you think your recipe for success is for each of the following areas. A "10" means you are very good at it; a "5" means you are OK at it; a "1" means you are not very good in this area.

Listener	10	9	8	7	6	5	4	3	2	1
Motivator	10	9	8	7	6	5	4	3	2	1
Chemist	10	9	8	7	6	5	4	3	2	1
Educator	10	9	8	7	6	5	4	3	2	1
Responsibility taker	10	9	8	7	6	5	4	3	2	1
Facilitator	10	9	8	7	6	5	4	3	2	1
Vision creator	10	9	8	7	6	5	4	3	2	1
Chef	10	9	8	7	6	5	4	3	2	1

5

Building Positive Relationships

Learning Emphasis
- Describe why attitude is important to a team.
- Outline ways to boost team attitudes for stronger relationships.
- List three reasons why it is important to build relationships.
- Describe two ways to maintain and strengthen relationships.

Time Required
- 60–90 minutes (depending on number of activities completed)

Materials Needed
- Relationship activities
- Pen/pencil for each participant
- Index cards—one per participant
- Participant journal (optional)
- Handouts U through Z

Activity Agenda
- Chapter Connection to Environmental Stewardship Project
- Good or Bad Activity
- Magnifying Glass Activity
- Karaoke Activity
- Bartering Activity
- Building Relationships Activity
- Exploring What We Learned Today

Chapter Connection to Environmental Stewardship Project

⇨ Facilitator Says: *"In this portion of our leadership program, we will be learning about building positive relationships. Remember that we will all be challenged at the end of the program with leading an environmental project. Attitude and relationship building are critical components of successful leadership. Participants who demonstrate a positive attitude and who are able to build positive relationships with others will be better prepared to cooperatively work with others to successfully complete an environmental stewardship project."*

Good or Bad Activity

⇨ Facilitator Says: *"Just about everyone had heard people talk about attitude. For example, our parents tell us, "You had better change that attitude!" At school, our teachers might tell us, "Well, if you would improve that attitude…" Society tells us, "Kids today just do not have the right attitude." So much is said about attitude that it can all get rather confusing. Is attitude a good thing or a bad thing? When I say 'Brainstorm,' turn to your neighbor. Spend a moment discussing whether attitude is a good thing or a bad thing. Stop talking when I say 'Stop.'"*

• Give participants a moment to discuss. Call on three to five pairs to share with the group.

⇨ Facilitator Says: *"Attitude is generally defined as a person's state of mind. And attitudes can be positive or negative. As we continue with our discussion about attitude, remember our discussion about how attitude can be a very good thing. Be dedicated young people committed to finding out how attitude can help enhance your abilities as a team leader and as a team player as we learn together today."*

Magnifying Glass Activity

⇨ Facilitator Says: *"Knowing about attitude is not enough. We interact with so many people in many different situations. This knowledge is best practiced when we work as part of a team."*

• Distribute one copy of Handout U to each participant. Provide the following instructions.

⇨ Facilitator Says: *"Write or draw why you believe attitude is important to a team."*

• Allow about one minute. When participants are ready to continue, ask them to share their ideas with a partner.

⇨ Facilitator Says: *"Attitude is important to a team because it…*
- ✓ *Allows work to get done.*
- ✓ *Provides for efficiency.*
- ✓ *Calls for all members to give their best.*
- ✓ *Draws on the various personalities represented to be successful."*

- Next, explore how attitudes are expressed here with a group discussion.

  ⇨ Facilitator Says: *"What are some examples (here in this program) where a positive attitude has made an activity or task easier to complete? When people show a positive attitude, what behaviors do you notice?"* (You may choose to use Handout V for participants to capture what they have observed.)

- Next, explore how leaders can boost attitudes.

  ⇨ Facilitator Says: *"If you were a leader here, what could you do to help boost the attitudes of people you were leading? Pick someone next to you to share your ideas."*

- Examples of attitude boosters are included in Handout W. These examples include:
  - ✓ Think of others first and self second.
  - ✓ Work for the good of the cause.
  - ✓ Seek team harmony.
  - ✓ Do not react to situations.
  - ✓ Actively listen to others.
  - ✓ Remember that change begins with you.

Karaoke Activity

- Break participants into small groups of four or five.

  ⇨ Facilitator Says: *"When we think of people who are the ultimate 'attitude boosters,' cheerleaders often come to mind. With their enthusiasm and pep, cheerleaders do their jobs well. Imagine that you are a cheerleading group. Create a song or a cheer that talks about the importance of having a positive attitude as a leader. You can create your own song/cheer or modify the words to an existing song/cheer you know. You can also come up with movements to go along with your cheer/ song."*

- Allow each team to perform its song/cheer.

  ⇨ Facilitator Says: *"It has been exciting uncovering the information about 'attitude.' Many people in the world seem to use the word so insignificantly in conversation, usually focusing on its negative aspects. As we have learned, attitude carries extraordinary power to boost a team's ability to work effectively and efficiently. As we live each day, let's continue to observe our behaviors and ensure they will have a positive effect on the attitudes of others."*

Bartering Activity

⇨ Facilitator Says: *"Today, we are going to learn the importance of building the relationships we already have and even some tips on how to start new relationships. Relationships start with the heart, so let's put our hearts and minds into our conversations about leadership today."*

• Participants will receive an index card with a statement on it. (Important: You will need to create the cards *before* this activity. These statements are on Handout X and can be printed off and taped or glued to an index card, with one statement per card.) Each participant will have about three minutes to find the person who has what he needs to be complete. For example, the situation on card A is a person who is being relocated to another state and card B is someone with a moving company. The object is for each participant to find his match so each side can achieve what is needed.

• Pass out the cards facedown.

⇨ Facilitator Says: *"Each of you have received a card. When I say 'Search,' find the person who may be able to help you based on the information on your card. Think about something you may need or want based on what you see on your card. After three minutes, I will say 'Freeze.' You will immediately go to your seat with your partner. What are your questions? 'Search.'"*

• Time participants for three minutes. At the end of three minutes, say "Freeze."

⇨ Facilitator Says: *"'Freeze.' Please find a seat with your partner, and we will discuss the benefits of building the relationship you just discovered."*

• Process the activity with the following question.

⇨ Facilitator Says: *"What other situations can you think of where you have needed someone's help?"*

• Brainstorm out loud with all participants. (Example response from participant: "When we were moving into the cabin/lodge on the first day of camp, I needed help carrying my bags or making my bed.")

Building Relationships Activity

⇨ Facilitator Says: *"Now that we have thought about situations in which we would help others, let's talk more about relationship building. What are some reasons we may want to build relationships? Think about different aspects of your life and the different types of relationships you might want to develop."* (You may choose to use Handout Y with this activity.)

• If participants come up with more answers, write them on the flip chart.

⇨ Facilitator Says: *"Now that we know the reasons we have relationships, let's think about some ways we can maintain and strengthen those relationships. Think for a moment about a relationship in your life that may need attention or work. Once you have that relationship in mind, take another moment to think about something you could do to make the relationship better—to strengthen it."*

• Wait about one to two minutes for participants to have their ideas, then proceed.

⇨ Facilitator Says: *"Let's talk about some of the relationships that need attention. You do not need to tell us the relationship (but you can if you choose); instead, share some way you plan to work on the relationship."*

• Call on volunteers to answer the question. (See Handout Z for answers.)

Exploring What We Learned Today

The following OPTIONS are designed (a) to provide participants with more reflection opportunities, (b) to provide facilitators with a method to assess learning, and (c) to provide additional opportunities for learning to be applied. Facilitators may choose to complete *one or more of the options* from the following list based on time available and the overall goals of your organization's leadership and environmental stewardship program.

• OPTION 1: In your journals, write down the three most important things you learned about attitude. Describe the impact you believe this information will have on your effectiveness as a member or leader of a team. Be sure to think about positive behaviors, attitude boosters, and why attitude is important. Share your work with one member of the group.

• OPTION 2: Process the Relationships chapter by using the following questions:
  ✓ Name three reasons it is important to build relationships.
  ✓ Describe two ways to strengthen relationships.

• OPTION 3: Have participants create a personal goal related to their own attitudes. They should display this goal on their mirror and consult it each morning for a week, mentally referring to it throughout the day to keep the goal fresh. At the end of one week, have participants write a reflection in their journals, discussing the result of their goal as well as how (their attitude) improved, worsened, or stayed the same.

Handout U: I Know!

INSTRUCTIONS: On the magnifying glass below, write or draw why you believe attitude is important to a team. Turn your sheet over when finished, signaling your readiness to continue.

iStockphoto/Thinkstock

Handout V: Attitude Observation

INSTRUCTIONS: Take a few moments to record some easily observed behaviors that identify an attitude as "positive." Be sure to include where you saw those behaviors being exhibited.

Behavior	Where observed?	How does the behavior show a positive attitude?
_____	_____	_____
_____	_____	_____
_____	_____	_____
_____	_____	_____
_____	_____	_____
_____	_____	_____
_____	_____	_____
_____	_____	_____
_____	_____	_____
_____	_____	_____
_____	_____	_____
_____	_____	_____
_____	_____	_____
_____	_____	_____
_____	_____	_____
_____	_____	_____

Handout W:
Ways to Boost
Attitudes as a Leader

- Think of others first and self second.

- Work for the good of the cause.

- Seek team harmony.

- Do not react to situations.

- Actively listen to others.

- Remember that change begins with you.

Handout X: Bartering Cards

Barter Activity Descriptions for Cards

(A) You own a moving truck.

(B) You are moving to a new state and need someone to help with the move.

(A) You love vacationing in Aspen, Colorado, where ski resorts are everywhere. The problem is you do not know how to ski!

(B) You are a ski instructor who is just starting a business. You need clients!

(A) You have a brand-new iPod, but your iTunes account has no songs in it.

(B) You have an iTunes account with lots of songs, but your iPod is broken.

(A) You have an emergency and need to call home but do not have a phone.

(B) You have a cell phone and usually let your friends make a call when they have an emergency.

(A) You have some wonderful desserts to share but no meal to go with them.

(B) You fixed a huge meal but have no dessert.

(A) You have an awesome car. Only one problem: You have no license!

(B) You have a driver's license, but you need a car.

(A) You lost your dog.

(B) You found a dog.

(A) You are traveling to France, but you do not know the language.

(B) You are a high school French facilitator.

(A) Your car is broken down.

(B) You received an "A" in automotive technology.

(A) You forgot your sweatshirt for gym class.

(B) You have a "closet" in your locker and always have an extra T-shirt or sweatshirt.

(A) You are a new student in high school.

(B) You are a high school guidance counselor who helps transfer students.

Handout Y:
Ways to Build
a Relationship

- Friendship and companionship (school friends, church friends, club friends, teammates)

- Work or professional (boss, supervisors, coworkers)

- Community activities and involvement (youth groups, volunteer opportunities)

- Mutual interests between people (someone with a common interest or hobby, such as dance team, camp, choir, spending time outdoors, sports/athletics, music)

Handout Z:
Ideas for Strengthening
a Relationship

- Take time out. Make time for the people who matter most to you. Share your time with others who may need someone to care about them.

- Do the little things that matter most. Send notes, make phone calls, and stay in touch with friends and family.

- Attend activities and events together. Spend time doing mutual hobbies (movies, music, sports, youth groups, traveling) with someone you consider a friend.

- Have meaningful conversations. Topics may include world issues, religion, and traveling.

6

Service

Learning Emphasis
- Define service as it relates to helping others.
- Illustrate attitudes and activities of service.
- Identify needs in camp, families, schools, and communities.
- Explore examples of environmental service opportunities connected to needs.

Time Required
- 60–90 minutes (depending on number of activities completed)

Materials Needed
- Service activities
- Pen/pencil for each participant
- Flip chart
- Map of your facility
- Large pieces of paper or poster board
- Markers
- Masking tape or pushpins for hanging posters
- Participant journal (optional)
- Handouts AA through GG

Activity Agenda
- Chapter Connection to Environmental Stewardship Project
- People Who Help Me Activity
- Defining Service Activity
- Quotations Poster Activity
- Binoculars Activity
- N.A.T.U.R.E. Service Activity
- Exploring What We Learned Today

Chapter Connection to Environmental Stewardship Project

⇨ Facilitator Says: *"In this portion of our leadership program, we will be learning about service and citizenship. Remember that we will all be challenged at the end of the program with leading an environmental project. Participants who understand the importance of service and how service is related to identified community needs will be better prepared and able to serve others in a leadership role. These skills improve the likelihood of project implementation in the participants' communities after they complete your program."*

People Who Help Me Activity

- Participants are going to be thinking about who helps them around camp. (If your organization is not a camp, you can adapt this activity as needed.) On a piece of paper (or in their journals), participants will list as many people as they can think of who help participants, the camp staff, the camp directors, or the surrounding community and how they do so. For example, the bus driver who drove participants to the camp (may not apply to your organization), the kitchen staff who cook meals and clean up the dining hall, the lifeguards who help at the pool, etc.

    ⇨ Facilitator Says: *"Let's all think about our camp. Raise your hand if you arrived at this facility by bus. You may put your hands down. Now raise your hand if you ate breakfast here. Okay, hands down. How many of you ever used our restrooms? Who swam in the pool this week? Have we ever stopped to think about the people who make it possible for us to do these things? Every day, we interact with many people who help us in some way."*

    ⇨ Facilitator Says: *"Today, we are going to take a little walk. This is a very special walk of remembering. Every day, each of us interacts with someone who helps us. Our mission is to identify those people and places where we are served. We are going to take a tour of the camp and capture in our journals every place and every person who has helped or served us in the past week or camp session. Are there any questions?"*

- Alternative Activity: If taking a walk around your site is not feasible, divide participants into groups of three or four and then provide each group with a site map. Give participants 10 to 15 minutes to identify areas where they are helped or served (and who helps them in those areas). Share findings as a group.

- After participants return from their site walk (or their review of the site map), compile a master list on a flip chart of people who serve them and places where they are served. Discuss the following questions with participants.

⇨ Facilitator Says: *"What did we just do? Why should we care about people who help us?"*

　✓ Participants' responses might include: because they make our lives easier; they sacrifice their own time to make us better people; we take them for granted sometimes; etc.

⇨ Facilitator Says: *"Why is recognizing how much we are served every day and how it makes a difference in our lives important? What does this have to do with learning how to be a leader?"*

• Solicit feedback from participants.

⇨ Facilitator Says: *"We all need help sometimes, and we all have the ability to help others. We have just identified many examples of people who serve us. Let's explore how we can help others by being of service."*

Defining Service Activity

⇨ Facilitator Says: *"Based on the activity we just completed about who helps us, take 30 seconds to think about your own definition of service. You can write it down if you want. If it is helpful to include an example, jot that down too. Be ready to share your definitions."*

• Allow about 15 seconds for participants to write down the definition of service. Call on participants randomly to share their ideas. Then, share Handout AA.

⇨ Facilitator Says: *"These are all great examples and definitions of service. However, the definition of service we will be using today is: Service is making a difference in someone else's life by helping to meet a need. Service is contributing to the well-being of others through actions of helpfulness."*

• Discuss what this definition means by tying it to the acts of helpfulness generated from the service walk (or the service discussion from the site map).

⇨ Facilitator Says: *"Give me some examples from our service walk (or the service discussion from the site map) of someone who was meeting a need through helpfulness."*

• Discuss participants' answers.

⇨ Facilitator Says: *"Anyone can perform actions that help people, but service is more than just actions. Think about what we learned about building positive relationships. Service also includes attitude."*

Quotations Poster Activity

- Break participants into groups of three or four. Give each group a copy of Handout BB (quotation about service). Have the group discuss the quotation and then create a poster illustrating the quotation.

  ⇨ Facilitator Says: *"We are going to look at some famous quotations related to service. These quotations say a lot about what our attitude toward service should be. Our challenge is to create a poster that illustrates each quotation."*

- Pass out poster board and markers. While some of the quotations may seem abstract, participants can use their creativity to express the attitude conveyed by the quotation. Give participants time to make their posters and then bring them back together as a large group. Have each group take about one minute to share its poster with the group, explaining the meaning of the quotation. Tape or pin the posters so they are visible to all participants. Discuss them with participants.

  ⇨ Facilitator Says: *"What have we learned about attitude from these quotations? How does attitude affect our actions of service?"*

- Have participants think back to the service walk (or their review of the site map) to identify three people they can serve or three ways they can serve (this week or during this program session). They should capture this in their journals.

  ⇨ Facilitator Says: *"Thinking back to the service walk (or our review of the site map), let's switch our thinking and connect service to action. Instead of thinking how we are served, think about how we can serve others. In your notes, write down three ways you can serve someone this week (or during this session)."*

Binoculars Activity

  ⇨ Facilitator Says: *"Picture your camp, family, school, or community. Your challenge for this activity is to think about the things in your lives you do not always notice or do not always see, mostly because you overlook them. We are going to help each other identify the needs that are hidden in our camp, families, school, and communities and then work together as a team to identify opportunities to meet those needs through service."*

- Cup your hands around your eyes, like you are looking through a pair of binoculars. Ask participants to do the same.

  ⇨ Facilitator Says: *"Everyone, imagine you are looking through a pair of binoculars. Hold them up to your eyes. You are now a Needs Explorer—on the hunt for hidden needs in your families, schools, and communities. Turn to a partner with your mental binoculars and say, 'Let the adventure begin!'"*

⇨ Facilitator Says: *"Who knows what a need looks like? Do all needs look the same? Some may be so big that we run right into them, while others may be so small that we need a magnifying glass. What do I mean when I say the word needs? Think to yourself about other words or phrases that describe needs, and be ready to give an example."*

• Call on several participants to give their examples and then share Handout CC.

⇨ Facilitator Says: *"Needs can be the lack of something necessary, desirable, or useful; physical or mental requirements for one's well-being or survival; or conditions requiring relief. Now that we know what needs are, let's think about the needs of people around us."*

• Distribute Handout DD on identifying the needs of your family, community, and school.

⇨ Facilitator Says: *"Look at the table on Handout DD. You can see four columns that represent your camp, family, school, and community. Put on your memory binoculars again and think about the past few months. Try to recall different needs you have seen or even felt in your camp, family, school, and community. Take a minute to list these on your sheet."*

• Using a flip chart, list and discuss what participants came up with. Combine the needs that were discovered to create one list.

⇨ Facilitator Says: *"How does it make you feel to know so many needs are out there? What can we do about these needs? Do we have the ability and/or responsibility to help?"*

• Have a discussion to help participants understand they can take action to help.

⇨ Facilitator Says: *"Remember our definition of service? Service is making a difference in someone else's life by helping to meet a need. Service is contributing to the well-being of others through our actions of helpfulness. When we take action to help meet the needs of others, we are performing acts of service. When we perform acts of service, we are demonstrating leadership in our camps, homes, schools, and communities."*

N.A.T.U.R.E. Service Activity

• Participants will break into teams of four or five to complete the next activity. As you explain directions, hand out copies of Handout EE.

⇨ Facilitator Says: *"Many opportunities exist for us to serve. In fact, every need you discovered is like a clue or a link to another opportunity. Now let's brainstorm opportunities for environmental service. Take a look at the grid on Handout EE."*

⇨ Facilitator Says: *"Along the left-hand side of this grid, you can see the categories of needs we established earlier: family, school, and community. Along the top of the grid are the letters N, A, T, U, R, and E, which describe what services we can do for the environment. Brainstorm service opportunities in each of the four categories (camp, family, school, and community) that begin with the letters at the top (the letters N, A, T, U, R, and E). Use the lists you created on Handout DD to help you brainstorm. The opportunities for service can be large or small and can include ideas you would address alone or as part of a group. In small groups of four or five participants, take 10 minutes to complete the grid. When you are finished, raise your hand. Any questions?"*

- Have selected groups report back and then capture the ideas on a flip chart. Pay close attention to the service ideas that relate to environmental service.

⇨ Facilitator Says: *"Wow! You have found many opportunities for service! However, our purpose is not only just to identify opportunities but to also take action!"*

- Give each participant a copy of Handout FF. Participants will choose one activity (from their N.A.T.U.R.E. service grid) they can complete in the next 48 hours and make a plan by answering the first four questions. (They will complete the final six questions after their service.) The activities the participants choose may be related to their experience here in this program or they might be family, school, or community focused if they will be returning home sometime in the next 48 hours.

⇨ Facilitator Says: *"Obviously, we cannot do everything on this list right away, but we do not have to wait for big moments to serve others; we can start tonight with small things. Look at the service grid we just completed and choose two opportunities you can address in the next 48 hours. Then, circle or place a star by your choices."*

⇨ Facilitator Says: *"You are going to take the next five minutes to create a service plan for these activities. Use Handout FF to draw a picture or write a description of the service you plan to do. Tomorrow, after you have completed the acts of service, you can turn in these coupons to earn a special prize."*

- Give participants about five minutes to create their plan for their service activity. (Optional: You can choose to have participants use Handout GG as a coupon to verify their service.) Have some type of nominal prize, such as stickers or candy, to give to participants when they turn in their coupons over the next two days.

- Be sure to give participants time in a couple of days to reflect back on the service they provided and to answer questions 4 through 10 on Handout FF.

Exploring What We Learned Today

The following OPTIONS are designed (a) to provide participants with more reflection opportunities, (b) to provide facilitators with a method to assess learning, and (c) to provide additional opportunities for learning to be applied. Facilitators may choose to complete *one or more of the options* from the following list based on time available and the overall goals of your organization's leadership and environmental stewardship program.

- OPTION 1: Draw an example lightbulb, smiley face, and hand icon on a flip chart. Direct participants' attention to the flip chart and then ask the following review questions:
  - ✓ Lightbulb—What was the main idea or "a-ha" you learned from this activity?
  - ✓ Smiley face—What is your attitude about service and has it changed from the beginning of the activity?
  - ✓ Hand—What actions of service are you going to take to help others?

- OPTION 2: Have participants choose one person (here in this program) who is known for helping or serving others. Ask participants to write in their journals about how that person has been a good example of a leader involved in service.

- OPTION 3: As a follow-up to the N.A.T.U.R.E. activity, have participants break into groups of four or five to share their experiences. As a group, they can pick one experience to share with the entire group. Set up the room like a TV station, with each group pretending to be a news team. Have each team present a skit that shares the results of their service activities.

- OPTION 4: Assess what participants learned in this chapter by using the following questions.

True or False

_____ Service is making a difference in someone else's life by helping to meet a need.

_____ Attitude is all in the way that you walk and talk.

_____ Service is contributing to the well-being of others through our actions of helpfulness.

_____ A need is a lack of something necessary, desirable, or useful.

_____ Few opportunities exist to serve in my family, school, and community.

Short Answer

- Give two examples of service projects that meet needs.

- How does attitude affect our actions and service to others?

Handout AA: What Is Service?

Service is making
a difference in
someone else's life
by helping to meet a need.

Service is contributing to
the well-being of others
through actions of
helpfulness.

Handout BB:
Quotations on the
Benefits of Service

"I don't know what your destiny will be, but one thing I know: the ones among you who will be really happy are those who have sought and found how to serve."

—Albert Schweitzer

"Great works do not always lie in our way, but every moment we may do little ones excellently, that is, with great love."

—St. Francis de Sales

"Everyone can be great...because anybody can serve. You don't have to have a college degree to serve. You don't have to make your subjects and verbs agree to serve. You only need a heart full of grace, a soul generated by love."

—Rev. Dr. Martin Luther King Jr.

"I long to accomplish a great and noble task, but it is my chief duty to accomplish small tasks as if they were great and noble."

—Helen Keller

"If anyone desires to be first, he should be last of all and servant to all."

—Jesus

"No one can sincerely try to help another without helping himself."

—Unknown

Handout CC:
What Are Needs?

Needs are:

- The lack of something necessary, desirable, or useful

- Physical or mental requirements for one's well-being or survival

- Conditions that require relief

- Family

- School

- Community

Handout DD: Needs in My Camp, Family, School, and Community

INSTRUCTIONS: Brainstorm needs you have seen or even felt in your camp, family, school, and community.

Camp	Family	School	Community

Handout EE: Opportunities for Service Grid

INSTRUCTIONS: Brainstorm service opportunities in each of the four categories (camp, family, school, and community) that begin with the letters at the top (the letters N, A, T, U, R, and E). Use the lists you created on Handout DD to help you brainstorm. The opportunities for service can be large or small and can include ideas you would address alone or as part of a group. Try to incorporate at least one or two ideas that involve helping the environment. Examples are provided for each category.

	N.A.T.U.R.E. *(Service ideas that begin with N, A, T, U, R, or E)*
Camp	Example: Nail down loose boards at the waterfront area.(Starts with "N")
Family	Example: Take food donations to the homeless shelter with my family. (Starts with "T")
School	Example: Accept responsibility to mentor a friend who needs help with advanced math. (Starts with "A")
Community	Example: Recycle cell phones in my neighborhood. (Starts with "R")

Handout FF: My Service Activity

(Before) Preservice

1. Date of activity:

2. What is the need?

3. What is the act of service?

4. What do I expect to happen?

(After) Postservice

5. What actually happened?

6. Was I able to meet the need?

7. Did anyone else know about it?

8. If so, how did they respond? How did they feel?

9. How did I feel?

10. What did I learn about myself from this act of service?

Handout GG: Coupon for My Service Activity

_____ 's Service Coupon

(your name)

Good for one act of service to: _____

(person or group you will help)

for _____ on _____ .

(What is the need?)   (date you will be providing service)

Signed: _____

(Signature of person or group you helped)

7

Taking Initiative

Learning Emphasis
- Define the qualities of a self-starter.
- Identify qualities of an independent worker.
- Assess his qualities and shortcomings when working independently.

Time Required
- 30–60 minutes (depending on number of activities completed)

Materials Needed
- Initiative activities
- Pen/pencil for each participant
- Flip chart
- Battery-powered drill with screwdriver attachment (if available)
- Phillips-head screwdriver (if available)
- Participant journal (optional)
- Handouts HH through JJ

Activity Agenda
- Chapter Connection to Environmental Stewardship Project
- Screwdriver Activity
- Being a Self-Starter Activity
- Independence Activity
- Eyewitness News Self-Assessment Activity
- Exploring What We Learned Today

Chapter Connection to Environmental Stewardship Project

⇨ Facilitator Says: *"In this portion of our leadership program, we will be learning about taking initiative and being a self-starter. Remember that we will all be challenged at the end of the program with leading an environmental project. Many environmental problems require leaders who are willing and able to take initiative. Participants who understand the importance of self-motivation and who are able to work independently will be better prepared and able to start on a project. Providing participants with on-site experiences working independently is recommended."*

Screwdriver Activity

- Walk around the room, holding up a rechargeable drill with a Phillips-head bit. Simultaneously, pass around a conventional Phillips-head screwdriver.

  ⇨ Facilitator Says: *"Pay careful attention to the object being passed around the room. Also, examine carefully the object I am holding. Be prepared to answer some questions."*

  ⇨ Facilitator Says: *"What is the object that is being passed around the room? What is the object in my hand? Have you used either of these tools before? Most all of you have had some experience with one of these tools or have at least seen them used before. Today, you are going to use your knowledge of these simple tools to examine your own work habits and patterns."*

  ⇨ Facilitator Says: *"Think back to your own experiences with the two tools we have in our room. How have you used them? Take a few moments to think of when, where, and how you used these tools. Be ready to share your experience with the group."*

- Call on willing volunteers to share their experiences in using the tools. Ask questions to compare the ease of using the hand tool versus the power tool.

  ⇨ Facilitator Says: *"Which tool is easier to use to put screws in place: the power drill with the screwdriver bit or the one without the motor?"*

- Discuss participants' answers.

  ⇨ Facilitator Says: *"Why is the power tool easier to use?"*

- Discuss participants' responses.

⇨ Facilitator Says: *"Right—it did require less effort to use! You simply pushed a button and held it in place and it went to work, whereas the handheld screwdriver required you to twist and turn your hand."*

- Relate this to the participants' independent work.

  ⇨ Facilitator Says: *"Think for a second about your own work habits. Which tool best represents you? Are you the power tool or the hand tool? Take the next few minutes to answer these questions in your journals:*

  ✓ *Are you more like the power screwdriver or the screwdriver without the motor?*

  ✓ *Do you work easily on your own or does it take someone else's hard efforts to get you working?*

  ✓ *Are you a self-starter or does it take you some major encouragement to begin a new task?"*

- Call on volunteers to provide personal answers to the questions.

Being a Self-Starter Activity

⇨ Facilitator Says: *"All of you were able to identify with one of the tools. Some of you describe yourself as easy to start, while others realize that many times, it takes others to get you started. Today, we are going to look at what it takes to be a self-starter. You will also evaluate your own work habits and determine what you can do to become a self-starter. Let's now take our notebooks and capture the definition and some key points of a self-starter."*

- Share Handout HH (which contains the definition and qualities of a self-starter).

  ⇨ Facilitator Says: *"A self-starter is a person who is independently motivated to begin a task. Several qualities distinguish a self-starter from others who are not self-motivated. Self-starters work on tasks/projects independently. They have a sense of ownership and responsibility for tasks/projects. They are self-motivated. They usually focus on success and are committed until the task is completed."*

- Explore with participants the benefits of being a self-starter.

  ⇨ Facilitator Says: *"How do you know when a person is a self-starter? What characteristics does a self-starter exhibit? What does it look like when a person is not a self-starter?"*

- Pause and take participant responses. Then, ask participants to find a partner to talk about their experiences with being a self-starter.

  ⇨ Facilitator Says: *"Think of a time when you exhibited the qualities of a self-starter. What motivated you to begin and to successfully complete a task? What was the outcome? How were you and others involved in the project affected?"*

Independence Activity

⇨ Facilitator Says: *"We identified one of the major qualities of being a self-starter as the ability to work independently. Now let's point out the qualities that distinguish independence from reliance solely on others."*

• Pass out papers that list the qualities of independence (Handout II) and then give each participant a number from one to four depending on the number of groups you have. Several participants will receive a paper entitled "party host" and a number from one to four. Break participants into groups of five or six, matching up with the party hosts.

⇨ Facilitator Says: *"As you receive your slip of paper, read the quality listed on the paper, but do not show it to anyone. Think of a way to act out your quality. If your paper reads "party host," it will be your mission to guess what qualities the guests at your party possess. You also have a number at the bottom of your paper. As I call out your number, come to where I am standing to meet your group. When I say "Party on!" your party may begin. Remember, guests: You may talk and act out your quality, but you may not say any words appearing on the paper. Are there any questions? 'Party on!'"*

• Give participants a few minutes to mingle around the room, acting out their characteristics. When enough time has passed, continue.

⇨ Facilitator Says: *"Good job, everyone! Let's review what the qualities of independence are when we put them all together."* (You can refer to Handout II.). *A person who is independent has the following characteristics:*
  ✓ *Self-motivated*
  ✓ *Begins tasks without assistance from others*
  ✓ *Follows through with tasks until completion*
  ✓ *Solves problems on his own*
  ✓ *Seeks advice and assistance only when needed"*

Eyewitness News Self-Assessment Activity

⇨ Facilitator Says: *"Let's find out how well each of us works independently."*

• Distribute Handout JJ. Ask each participant to find a partner. Use the Eyewitness News approach (where one participant interviews his partner and then they switch roles after a few minutes) to retrieve participant answers to these questions.

⇨ Facilitator Says: *"Using the questions you have in front of you, rely on your investigative skills to determine what kind of independent worker your partner is. When you are the reporter, write down your witness's responses to the questions on your page. Then, give your question-and-answer page to the person you interviewed."*

Exploring What We Learned Today

The following OPTIONS are designed (a) to provide participants with more reflection opportunities, (b) to provide facilitators with a method to assess learning, and (c) to provide additional opportunities for learning to be applied. Facilitators may choose to complete *one or more of the options* from the following list based on time available and the overall goals of your organization's leadership and environmental stewardship program.

- OPTION 1: Ask participants to look for examples of self-starters during the rest of the day (here in this program) and be prepared to share tomorrow. Participants can write what they observe in their journals.

- OPTION 2: Ask participants the following questions:
  ✓ What are the benefits and challenges of being a self-starter?
  ✓ What actions can be taken to overcome these challenges?
  ✓ What are the benefits and challenges of being an independent worker?
  ✓ What actions can be taken to overcome these challenges?

- OPTION 3: Ask participants to reflect on what it means to be a self-starter and independent worker by writing a newspaper article about someone who exhibits these qualities.

- OPTION 4: Ask participants to answer the following questions (either aloud as a group or in their journals).
  ✓ Which of the following are qualities of a self-starter?
    - Self-motivated
    - Success oriented
    - Commitment until completion
    - Dependent on others to finish task
  ✓ An independent leader can be best described as:
    - An unmotivated person who relies on others to complete tasks
    - A self-motivated person who follows through with tasks until their completion
    - An unmotivated person who follows through with tasks until their completion
    - A self-motivated person who relies on others to complete tasks

- OPTION 5: Ask participants to think about the N.A.T.U.R.E. service activity they previously identified. How will being a self-starter be important for completion of their service activity? In what ways will they need to be a self-starter? (Or in what ways were they a self-starter?)

Handout HH:
Qualities of a Self-Starter

Self-Starter

- A person who is independently motivated to begin a task

Qualities of a Self-Starter

- Works on tasks/projects independently

- Holds a sense of ownership and responsibility

- Is self-motivated

- Focuses on success

- Is committed until the task is completed

Handout II:
Qualities of Being Independent

- Is self-motivated

- Begins tasks without assistance from others

- Follows through with tasks until completion

- Solves problems on his own

- Seeks advice and assistance only when needed

Handout JJ:
How Well Do You Work Independently?

YES NO Do you complete any chores at home on a daily basis? *Why or why not?*

YES NO Do you complete homework assignments and turn them in on time? *Why or why not?*

YES NO Do you begin new tasks on your own? *Why or why not?*

YES NO Do you complete every task you begin? *Why or why not?*

YES NO When you have a problem with a homework question, do you seek help? *Why or why not?*

YES NO When you begin a task, do you become easily sidetracked by events going on around you? *Why or why not?*

YES NO Do you feel a sense of accomplishment when you complete a task you chose to begin? *Why or why not?*

YES NO Do you feel a sense of accomplishment when you complete a homework assignment? *Why or why not?*

YES NO Do you feel a sense of accomplishment when you complete your daily chores? *Why or why not?*

YES NO Are you responsible for the success and completion of a task you begin? *Why or why not?*

8

Setting and Achieving Goals

Learning Emphasis
- Define S.M.A.R.T. goals.
- Apply S.M.A.R.T. goal-setting techniques to environmental issues.
- Explore reasons why people do not achieve their goals.
- Discuss how to plan for goals.
- Identify resources for achieving goals.
- Create a written plan for personal goals.

Time Required
- 60–90 minutes (depending on number of activities completed)

Materials Needed
- Goal-setting activities
- Pen/pencil for each participant
- Flip chart
- Yellow paper plate
- Index cards (five for each participant)
- Blindfold
- Participant journal (optional)
- Handouts KK through QQ

Activity Agenda
- Chapter Connection to Environmental Stewardship Project
- Yellow Plate Race Activity
- Get S.M.A.R.T. Activity
- Creating a S.M.A.R.T. Environmental Goal Activity
- Quotes Activity
- Index Card Activity
- Blindfolded Walk Activity
- Goal-Setting Plan Activity
- Exploring What We Learned Today

Chapter Connection to Environmental Stewardship Project

⇨ Facilitator Says: *"In this portion of our leadership program, we will be learning about setting and achieving goals. Remember that we will all be challenged at the end of the program with leading an environmental project. An understanding of goal setting is essential for leadership, and successful leadership actions often require a plan. Understanding how to successfully develop a plan based on specific goals is a skill set that will lead directly into participants' development of their environmental stewardship project. Participants who understand the importance of setting clear and specific goals will be better able to plan and implement realistic stewardship projects."*

Yellow Plate Race Activity

- Take participants to an open area (inside or outside) and have them form a circle. Place a yellow plate in the center of the circle. The participants' goal is to select a partner and then switch places with the partner as quickly as possible. Time their efforts, and encourage the group to complete the challenge faster the second time.

  ⇨ Facilitator Says: *"In a minute, everyone will select a partner across the circle. Your goal is to touch the plate in the center of the circle and then switch places with your partner as quickly as possible without touching anyone in the process—not even your partner! While in motion, say 'Let's switch!' like you mean it, until you have reached your partner's position. When I say 'Start,' you may move. When everyone has reached his new position, someone else must say 'Stop!' Any questions? 'Start!'"*

- Time the group on its first attempt and then challenge the group to reduce its time on the second attempt. Have the participants think specifically about how fast they can complete the challenge. If their time is more than five seconds, share with them that many other groups have finished in less than one-and-a-half seconds. Participants should realize they can move closer to the spot or move the spot and do not have to be across from their partner.

- After participants have made their second attempt, discuss the following question.

  ⇨ Facilitator Says: *"What happened the first time?"*
    ✓ Possible responses: We did not understand what was going on; we did not think through our plan; we did not have a goal to aim for.

⇨ Facilitator Says: *"What was the difference the second time?"*

✓ Possible responses: We knew what we had to do to meet our time; we had the experience to draw from; our goal was clear.

⇨ Facilitator Says: *"What happened when the goal was not clear the first time?"*

✓ Possible responses: We did not use the best strategy to reach our end result; we were moving in chaos; we had nothing to shoot for.

⇨ Facilitator Says: *"How can you relate that to your life and becoming an effective leader?"*

✓ Possible responses: Without a goal, we will not exactly know where we are going; goals have to be specific to be helpful.

⇨ Facilitator Says: *"Many times in our lives, we feel like we are working toward something but are not quite sure what the result will be. Or maybe we know what the result will be, but we are just not sure how to reach the end point. Today, we are going to focus on goals and how we can use goal setting as we become effective leaders. Let's begin!"*

Get S.M.A.R.T. Activity

⇨ Facilitator Says: *"Today, I am going to share a tool with you that will make you five times smarter."*

• Share Handout KK.

⇨ Facilitator Says: *"All leaders develop goals when they are trying to complete a task or project. As you develop your goals or you work with others toward a goal, you should develop goals that are S.M.A.R.T.:*

✓ *Specific—explicitly set forth; definite. Goals must be specific. If goals are set and are not specific, it is impossible to judge whether we reach them. An example of an unspecific goal: I will exercise more. An example of a specific goal: I will exercise 20 minutes three times a week.*

✓ *Measurable—can be measured or calculated. Goals must be measurable. Measurable goals will help you evaluate your progress and measure your success. An example of an immeasurable goal: I will meet new people. An example of a measurable goal: I will attend four activities each month and introduce myself to at least one person I do not know.*

✓ *Approved by you—considered and consented to by you. Your goals must be set and approved by you. If you set your own goals, your chance of success will increase. Example: This means you want to be a successful leader for yourself, not because someone else wants you to.*

✓ *Realistic—tending to or expressing an awareness of things as they really are. Goals must be realistic. Setting goals you have the potential to achieve will help you follow through. Example: I will run a marathon next week with no training; versus: I will run a marathon after six months of intensive training.*

✓ *Time-stamped—established within a time frame. Goals have to have a time stamp. By setting and writing your deadlines down, you will start to live your goals. Example: I will visit my grandmother; versus: I will visit my grandmother by the end of the week."*

• After the S.M.A.R.T. framework is presented to participants, divide participants into groups of two and then ask them to create gestures, hand motions, or actions to represent each piece of the S.M.A.R.T. framework. After allowing a few minutes for participants to work on this in pairs, select a couple of pairs to demonstrate their gestures/hand motions/actions.

Creating a S.M.A.R.T. Environmental Goal Activity

⇨ Facilitator Says: *"We are learning about how to become leaders who are able to address environmental problems. Next, we are going to think about how to set goals that will help us solve environmental problems. Remember, our goals must be our own. Please remember to be respectful of other participants' ideas as we apply S.M.A.R.T. goals to nature-based problems or issues that are important to us. Let me know if you have any questions."*

• If participants struggle to identify environmental or nature-based problems to address, you may want to give them some ideas from the list in Handout GGG in Chapter 11.

• Distribute Handout LL and read the instructions aloud. Allow 10 minutes for participants to develop a S.M.A.R.T. goal.

⇨ Facilitator Says: *"Use Handout LL to identify one S.M.A.R.T. goal for an environmental or nature-based problem or issue that is important to you. This activity is about practice. Do not worry about being perfect. Focus on the different parts of a S.M.A.R.T. goal and how your environmental problem can be described by using each part."*

• Ask selected participants to share what they developed. Remind participants that this activity was about practicing with the S.M.A.R.T. framework.

⇨ Facilitator Says: *"Unfortunately, setting S.M.A.R.T. goals is not enough. Just because you set goals that are S.M.A.R.T. does not mean you will achieve them. Can you think of some reasons why people might not achieve their goals?"*

• Solicit ideas from participants and then share Handout MM.

⇨ Facilitator Says: *"Those are good ideas. The following are some other reasons why goals might fail. People set goals that are too big. Goals are not written down or planned. Their fear of failure leads to a fear to start. They do it alone. Let's think about each of these challenges one at a time. People do not achieve their goals because:*

✓ *One, they set goals that are too big. You should be sure to make goals that are bite sized. Instead of setting a goal to get better grades in all classes, set a goal to make better grades in two classes.*

✓ *Two, goals are not written down or planned. It is a proven fact that a written goal carries more power. Writing your goal forces you to be specific and think through all your actions.*

✓ *Three, fear of failure leads to a fear to start. Many people are too afraid they will fail, so they never start working toward their goals. They do not want to commit the time and energy without the guarantee of success. However, life has no guarantees, so just go for it!*

✓ *Four, they go it alone. When setting goals, borrow strength from people around you. You should identify key individuals who can help you reach your goals. It could be a brother, a sister, a parent, a counselor, a grandparent, a pastor, etc. Find someone who will hold you accountable for reaching your goals."*

Quotes Activity

- Give one copy of Handout NN to each participant. Ask participants to find a partner to read the quotes on the handout with. As a team, they should identify how the quotes are similar (What do the quotes have in common?) and how the quotes are related to leadership.

- After a few minutes, elicit responses for the following questions.

  ⇨ Facilitator Says: *"What do these four quotes have in common?"*
  ✓ Possible responses: Planning, preparing, and achieving success.

  ⇨ Facilitator Says: *"What are the general themes among the quotes?"*
  ✓ Possible responses: Achieving your goal because of thinking beforehand; success depends on how much planning is done; you have to plan to be successful.

  ⇨ Facilitator Says: *"How can you relate these quotes to leadership?"*
  ✓ Possible responses: The more we plan, the better chance we will succeed as leaders; we have the ability to reach our goals by planning.

  ⇨ Facilitator Says: *"Think back to our discussions about goals. We know how to set S.M.A.R.T. goals, but what good are they if we do not have a plan to achieve them? Our goals are only as good as our plan to make them happen. As we dive into this topic, remember that you have the power. You have the power to make your goals your reality. So, what are we waiting for? Let's get started!"*

⇨ Facilitator Says: *"For example, let's say that the environmental problem that I identified was a lack of places for kids in my neighborhood to enjoy nature. My goal is to create a walking and hiking trail. First, I have to map out my goal by using the S.M.A.R.T. framework. Then, I have to identify all the steps I might have to complete to achieve my goal. I have to identify a place where a trail might be built. I have to determine who in my neighborhood can help me. And so on."*

Index Card Activity

⇨ Facilitator Says: *"Successfully achieving our goals can require completion of multiple steps, and we have to prioritize what we will tackle first, second, third, and so on. Prioritization is a key skill of goal setting and being a successful leader. Prioritization means to arrange or deal with in order of importance."*

- Give each participant five index cards. Then, ask the participants to look at the environmental goal they recently developed in the previous activity. Participants are to use the cards to break down their environmental goal into a series of steps. Participants will then sort the cards according to which task will come first, second, third, and so on. (If participants want to create a new goal because the environmental goal activity was focused on practice, then allow them to create a new goal. Be sure to remind them to follow the S.M.A.R.T. framework.)

⇨ Facilitator Says: *"Think about the environmental goal that you recently developed. I am going to give each of you five index cards. Use the cards to break down your environmental goal into a series of five steps. Next, you will sort the cards according to which task will come first, second, third, and so on. If your goal requires more than five steps, then I can give you additional index cards. Any questions?"*

- After enough time has passed, discuss the following questions.

⇨ Facilitator Says: *"What was difficult about this task?"*
  ✓ Possible responses: Hard to think through all the steps; not sure what the steps would be; all steps were equally important; could not decide which was more important.

⇨ Facilitator Says: *"How will this process help us determine how to begin to address our environmental goals?"*

Blindfolded Walk Activity

⇨ Facilitator Says: *"With goals set and steps for achieving our goals prioritized, we still have things to do to make sure we achieve our goals. To help demonstrate another way to reach our goals, we need to locate the oldest and wisest participant in the room. Your challenge is to find the person without speaking."*

- Once the oldest participant has been identified, bring that person to the front of the room. The participant will have two chances to walk from one side of the room to the other (or, if you are outside, to walk from one landmark to another, such as two trees) while blindfolded. The other participants may not assist or aid the participant in any way on the first trip (except to keep the participant from harming himself). However, on the second trip, the participant may select one individual from the group to assist him in his journey.

  ⇨ Facilitator Says: *"To the participant who is blindfolded: You will have two minutes to travel from this side of the room to the other. You may not receive any assistance from other participants. Any questions? Go!"*

- Be sure to watch for potential safety concerns. Remind the other participants that they may not help the participant move across the room. Call time when two minutes is up.

  ⇨ Facilitator Says: *"To the participant who is blindfolded: You were close to reaching your goal the first time. We know you will make it this time. To assist you, you may select someone to help guide you across the room. He may not touch you, but he can only verbally help you to the other side. Select your guide."*

- Wait for the participant to select his helper.

  ⇨ Facilitator Says: *"Ready? Go!"*

- Be sure to watch for potential safety concerns. Remind participants that only one person is to help his blindfolded partner across the room. The participant should make it across the room before two minutes is up.

- Discuss the following questions.

  ⇨ Facilitator Says (to the participant who was blindfolded): *"What made the first try difficult?"*
    ✓ Possible responses: Not being able to see; not having any help; having to go alone.

  ⇨ Facilitator Says (to the participant who was blindfolded): *"What made the second try easier?"*
    ✓ Possible responses: Having someone to guide; having support or assistance.

  ⇨ Facilitator Says (to the whole group): *"How does this relate to the goals we have set and our work as leaders to solve environmental issues or problems?"*
    ✓ Possible responses: We need people to guide us; having support and assistance will help us reach our goals.

⇨ Facilitator Says: *"In this activity, our volunteer needed additional support and help to reach the goal of getting across the room. We all need the same for the goals in our lives. We must find people who will support us and our goals. To accomplish any goal, we need the help and cooperation of many people. This could be family, friends, coworkers, or even certain community organizations."*

- In pairs, have participants identify resources in their lives that can help them achieve their environmental goals.

  ⇨ Facilitator Says: *"Take the next three minutes to create a list of people who will help you reach your goals. Capture your ideas on your notes page and be prepared to share those with the group."*

- When time is up, have each pair share the ideas it came up with. You may also choose to capture suggestions on a flip chart.

Goal-Setting Plan Activity

⇨ Facilitator Says: *"Developing our goals is important, but as we learned from the Quotes Activity, developing a plan for our goals is important for actually achieving them. This next step is taking our goals to the next level. Be prepared to truly focus on how you will go about reaching your goals."*

⇨ Facilitator Says: *"For each goal that is set, a detailed plan is needed to assist us along our way. This allows us to focus on the details of reaching our goals. Before we starting planning, let's take a closer look at what a plan actually is. A plan is a scheme, program, or method worked out beforehand for the accomplishment of a goal or objective."*

- Share Handout OO.

  ⇨ Facilitator Says: *"To accomplish our objectives or goals, we need to have a method worked out before we start working toward that goal. Goal-setting plans typically include the following parts:*
  ✓ *S.M.A.R.T. goal*
  ✓ *Date to achieve by*
  ✓ *Potential obstacles*
  ✓ *Who can help (resources)*
  ✓ *Things to do*
  ✓ *How I know the goal was achieved"*

- Walk through an example of a goal being set by using the goal-setting plan. Use an example participants can relate to rather easily. For example, getting an "A" on a math test. You may choose to use Handout PP.

  ⇨ Facilitator Says: *"When we develop a plan for our goals, the goal will be likely to be achieved. One of the most powerful tools for making a goal a reality is to write it down as you would like to see it in reality. Not only will this help you visualize your goals, but it will help you determine what you are willing to do to make them happen."*

- Have participants complete Handout SS to develop a plan for the environmental goal they identified earlier. After they have completed their plan, have them trade with a partner to check their understanding of the planning process.

  ⇨ Facilitator Says: *"You will have 10 minutes to develop a plan for the environmental goal you created earlier by using Handout SS. Think through all the steps of the goal-setting plan. When you have your plan completed, trade with a partner so he can check your plan for anything that might have been left out. What questions are there? Begin!"*

- Participants will develop their plan and then trade when they are finished.

Exploring What We Learned Today

The following OPTIONS are designed (a) to provide participants with more reflection opportunities, (b) to provide facilitators with a method to assess learning, and (c) to provide additional opportunities for learning to be applied. Facilitators may choose to complete *one or more of the options* from the following list based on time available and the overall goals of your organization's leadership and environmental stewardship program.

- OPTION 1: Ask participants to answer the following questions: What have I learned about goal setting? How will I use what I have learned? (You can talk about the questions as a group or ask participants to write answers in their journals.)

- OPTION 2: Encourage participants to identify three famous people who have overcome obstacles to achieve their goals.

- OPTION 3: Ask participants the following question: Goals must be written as S.M.A.R.T. What do the letters in S.M.A.R.T. mean? (The answer is Specific, Measurable, Approved by you, Realistic, Time-stamped.)

- OPTION 4: Have participants answer the following question in their journals: Why is developing a plan to achieve my goals important?

- OPTION 5: Have participants complete each sentence (out loud as a group or they could be written in their journals).

  ✓ One reason people do not reach their goals is because they set goals that are too
  _____ .

  ✓ Goals that are not _____ or planned may not be achieved.

  ✓ For some, a fear of _____ leads to a fear to start.

  ✓ Instead of looking for help, some decide to go it _____.

Handout KK:
S.M.A.R.T. Environmental Goals

- Specific—explicitly set forth; definite. Goals must be specific. If goals are set and are not specific, it is impossible to judge whether we reach them. An example of an unspecific goal: I will exercise more. An example of a specific goal: I will exercise 20 minutes three times a week.

- Measurable—can be measured or calculated. Goals must be measurable. Measurable goals will help you evaluate your progress and measure your success. An example of an immeasurable goal: I will meet new people. An example of a measurable goal: I will attend four activities each month and connect with one new person.

- Approved by you—considered and consented to by you. Your goals must be set and approved by you. If you set your own goals, your chance of success will increase. Example: This means that you want to be a successful leader for yourself, not because someone else wants you to.

- Realistic—tending to or expressing an awareness of things as they really are. Goals must be realistic. Setting goals you have the potential to achieve will help you follow through. Example: "I will run a marathon next week with no training" versus "I will run a marathon after six months of vigorous training."

- Time-stamped—established within a time frame. Goals have to have a time stamp. By setting and writing your deadlines down, you will start to live your goals. Example: "I will visit my grandmother" versus "I will visit my grandmother by the end of the week."

Handout LL:
Setting an Environmental S.M.A.R.T. Goal

INSTRUCTIONS: Use this handout to identify one S.M.A.R.T. goal for an environmental or nature-based problem or issue that is important to you. This activity is about practice. Do not worry about being perfect. Focus on the different parts of a S.M.A.R.T. goal and how your environmental problem can be described using each part.

Write out your goal: _____

1. *How is your goal "Specific"?*

2. *How is your goal "Measurable"?*

3. *How is your goal "Approved"?*

4. *How is your goal "Realistic"?*

5. *How is your goal related to "Time"?*

Handout MM: Why Goals Fail

People do not achieve their goals because:

#1: They set goals that are too big.

> You should be sure to make goals that are bite sized. Instead of setting a goal to get better grades in all classes, set a goal to make better grades in two classes.

#2: Their goals are not written down or planned.

> It is a proven fact that a written goal carries more power. Writing your goal forces you to be specific and think through all your actions.

#3: Fear of failure leads to a fear to start.

> Many people are too afraid they will fail, so they never start working toward their goals. They do not want to commit the time and energy without the guarantee of success. However, life has no guarantees, so just go for it!

#4: They go it alone.

> When setting and pursuing your goals, borrow strength from others. You should identify key people who can help you reach your goals. It could be a brother, a sister, a parent, a counselor, a grandparent, a pastor, etc. Find someone who will hold you accountable for reaching your goals.

Handout NN: Goal-Related Quotes

"Whatever failures I have known,
whatever errors I have committed,
whatever follies I have witnessed
in private and public life
have been the consequence
of action without thought."

—Bernard Baruch

"A good plan is like a road map:
It shows the final destination and
usually the best way to get there."

—H. Stanley Judd

"You win not by chance,
but by preparation."

—Roger Maris

"To be prepared is
half the victory."

—Miguel de Cervantes

Handout OO: Parts of a Goal-Setting Plan

This handout lists the parts of a goal-setting plan. Reminder: A "plan" is a scheme, program, or method worked out beforehand for the accomplishment of a goal or objective.

- S.M.A.R.T. goal

- Date to achieve by

- Potential obstacles

- Who can help (resources)

- Things to do

- How I know the goal was achieved

Handout PP:
Example of a Completed
Goal-Setting Plan

- **S.M.A.R.T. goal:** I will earn a 90% on my math test next Tuesday.

- **Date to achieve by:** next Tuesday.

- **Potential obstacles:** finding time to study, my desire to study, working each night, not understanding the concepts being tested.

- **Who can help (resources):** friends in my class, my math teacher, my tutor, my parents.

- **Things to do:** study each night for 30 minutes, spend two days this week after school with teacher or tutor, review the night before with friends or parents.

- **How I know the goal was achieved:** check final grade on the test

Handout QQ: My Goal-Setting Plan

INSTRUCTIONS: Create a goal-setting plan by using this handout.

- S.M.A.R.T. goal:

- Date to achieve by:

- Potential obstacles:

- Who can help me? What are my resources?

- Things I have to do:

- How I know the goal was achieved:

9

Problem Solving and Planning

Learning Emphasis
- Define problem solving.
- Identify steps in the problem-solving process.
- Practice solving nature-based problems.
- Identify solutions and strategies to solving problems.

Time Required
- 60–90 minutes (depending on number of activities completed)

Materials Needed
- Problem-solving activities
- Pen/pencil for each participant
- Flip chart
- Signs made for each step of the problem-solving process (six signs total)
- Participant journal (optional)
- Handouts RR through VV

Activity Agenda
- Chapter Connection to Environmental Stewardship Project
- Human Knot Activity
- Investigating Problem Solving Activity
- Job Interview Activity
- Composting Activity
- Strategic Thinking Activity
- Exploring What We Learned Today

Chapter Connection to Environmental Stewardship Project

⇨ Facilitator Says: *"In this portion of our leadership program, we will be learning about problem solving. Remember that we will all be challenged at the end of the program with leading an environmental project. Participants who are able to identify and perform the problem-solving steps as well as identify relevant resources to solve a problem project will be better prepared and able to plan and implement their environmental stewardship projects."*

Human Knot Activity

- Have participants form a large circle. The participants will then form a human knot and try to solve it.

   ⇨ Facilitator Says: *"In a moment, the group will attempt to solve the problem of a human knot. Find an open area, make a large circle, and then join hands with two other people across the circle from them. Good luck untangling your problem: the human knot. Let's begin."*

- Once complete, ask the following questions and solicit responses from those who raise their hands.

   ⇨ Facilitator Says: *"What are some ways we solved the problem of the human knot?"*
   ✓ Potential answers include: talking with one another; listening to one another; we tried different ways; we listened to someone who had done the activity before; we were open to others' ideas.

Investigating Problem Solving Activity

   ⇨ Facilitator Says: *"You did a great job solving the problem of the human knot. Today, we will look at the problem-solving process and some problem-solving strategies. But first, let's put on our problem-solving face and define the term problem solving. Problem solving is 'the process by which problems are identified and solved.'"*

- Use Handout RR if needed. Ask participants to repeat the definition to two people sitting/standing near them.

- Ask participants if they have ever used problem solving and to give a specific example.

   ⇨ Facilitator Says: *"If you have ever used problem solving before, stand up and give a specific example. Please tell us the problem and what you did to solve the problem."*

- Choose a few participants to share when they used problem solving.

  ⇨ Facilitator Says: *"Thank you for sharing such good examples. By the end of our time together today, you will all be standing because we all use problem solving all the time!"*

- Ask participants to brainstorm the steps in solving a problem on their own and to write them down in their notebooks.

  ⇨ Facilitator Says: *"Think about some of the examples you and your fellow participants just shared. Take 30 seconds to write down the steps you think are necessary to solve a problem. They do not have to be in any particular order. Hint: The first step is to identify the problem. Begin!"*

- Give participants time to complete the exercise and then have them share the results.

  ⇨ Facilitator Says: *"Share some steps you came up with to solve a problem."*

- Allow a few participants to share their lists.

  ⇨ Facilitator Says: *"Those were some great ideas. You will definitely see some of your ideas in the specific steps in the problem-solving process we will use from now on."*

Job Interview Activity

- Distribute Handout SS and review the six steps of the problem-solving process:
  - ✓ Identify the problem.
  - ✓ Collect all needed information.
  - ✓ Guess what the solution will be.
  - ✓ Test to see if your guess works.
  - ✓ See what the result is.
  - ✓ Retry until the wanted solution is reached.

- Allow a few participants to share their lists.

  ⇨ Facilitator Says: *"Those were some great ideas. You will definitely see some of your ideas in the specific steps in the problem-solving process we will use from now on."*

- Ask for six volunteers to come to the front to hold signs to be put in the correct order for the problem-solving process. Once participants are selected, give them the cards you created ahead of time by using Handout TT. They should be out of order. Enlist their help to line them up in the correct order.

⇨ Facilitator Says: *"In a moment, we will solve a problem by using the problem-solving process. Who will be my six volunteers? Raise your hand to volunteer."*

- Pick your six volunteers and have them come to the front of the area. Give them a step in the problem-solving process and have them stand in random order.

  ⇨ Facilitator Says: *"The six volunteers should come up. Each of you is being given a single step of the problem-solving process. Stand silently side by side facing us, and the group will place you in the correct order. Any questions?"*

- Answer any questions and then let them begin.
  - ✓ The incorrect order is:
    - Receive a rejection letter with no interview.
    - Receive a job offer.
    - Look at job listings online and in a newspaper.
    - Prepare more thoroughly for the application and interview processes.
    - Complete a second job application and earn a job interview.
    - Complete a job application.
  - ✓ The correct order is:
    - Look at job listings online and in a newspaper.
    - Complete a job application.
    - Receive a rejection letter with no interview.
    - Prepare more thoroughly for the application and interview processes.
    - Complete a second job application and earn a job interview.
    - Receive a job offer.
- Once the cards are in order, go to the next activity.

  ⇨ Facilitator Says: *"Using the problem-solving process, we can solve everyday problems we face."*

Composting Activity

- As a group, participants will be given a challenge to use the problem-solving process to solve a problem related to a fictional organization's composting practices.

  ⇨ Facilitator Says: *"Using the problem-solving process, we can chart or strategize how to solve a problem. Solve the following problem: The camp has just started a compost pile with lawn clippings, chopped leaves, kitchen waste, and shredded paper and newspapers. Composting provides nutrients and improves the soil when done properly. However, this compost pile is attracting such critters as raccoons and mice. The pile will not compost properly when critters are interfering with the breakdown of the materials. Your challenge is to use the problem-solving process to determine a solution for keeping the critters from interfering with the compost pile. Keep these questions in mind as you think through the process: Are all the materials in the compost pile deemed as acceptable compost items? Is our compost pile properly layered? What would be attracting the critters? How can we continue our composting without attracting critters or disturbing their habitat?"*

- Have the group brainstorm all possible alternatives for each step and then vote on the best option at each step. (Participants can be allowed to break up into small groups if that is how they prefer to organize for this activity.)

Strategic Thinking Activity

⇨ Facilitator Says: *"A key component of problem solving is strategy. As you were solving the previous composting problem, you were probably using some type of strategy and you may not have even realized you were doing it. Does anyone know the meaning of the term strategy?"*

- Solicit feedback from the group and then share Handout UU.

⇨ Facilitator Says: *"A strategy is a plan of action intended to create a solution to a specific problem. A few strategies are commonly used when a person is trying to solve problems. For example:*
  - ✓ *Define the problem—what is the problem you want to solve?*
  - ✓ *Analyze the problem—what makes this a problem?*
  - ✓ *Establish criteria to evaluate solutions—how would I like to solve this problem?*
  - ✓ *Propose solutions—what are the possible solutions?*
  - ✓ *Take action—what would be the best way to act on the solution I decided on?"*

  ⇨ Facilitator Says: *"Can you think of any other problem-solving strategies we should add to this list?"*

- Discuss participants' ideas for additional strategies.

  ⇨ Facilitator Says: *"Excellent! You know the steps for solving problems and discovering solutions to them. Now that you know these skills, let's put them to use as we solve a problem. Let's examine another problem together as a group and follow the strategies to help develop a solution to it."*

- Share Handout VV. The problem described in the handout is: The local landfill in your community is exhibiting some difficulties because of the amount of waste being produced in your community. The landfill was not expected to be at full capacity until the year 2025, but because of the excess waste that is being produced in the community, it is currently projected to be at full capacity within five years. One reason for the landfill filling quickly is the lack of an environmental stewardship program for the community. If such a plan were in place, this could help the community reduce, reuse, and recycle waste. One place that produces a lot of waste is your local school. Create possible solutions to help your school reduce, reuse, and recycle the waste produced by the student body. Utilize the five problem-solving strategies to help create possible solutions to this issue.

- Read the scenario presented on Handout VV out loud. Then, allow the participants to read it again to themselves. Begin to work through the strategies to solve the problem. Allow for participant input to help solve the problem using the problem-solving strategies. Work through each step with participants to demonstrate how the problem-solving strategies work.

  ⇨ Facilitator Says: *"Now that you have had the opportunity to read the scenario, let's follow the strategies to help solve our problem. What is the problem in this scenario?"*

- Allow participants to answer this question. (You may choose to write their comments on a flip chart.)

  ⇨ Facilitator Says: *"Great! Now let's analyze this problem. What makes this a problem?"*

- Allow participants to answer the question. (You may choose to write their comments on a flip chart.)

  ⇨ Facilitator Says: *"Very good! Let's establish the criteria as to how we would evaluate our solution."*

- Allow participants to answer the question. (You may choose to write their comments on a flip chart.)

  ⇨ Facilitator Says: *"Okay, what is the purpose of our solution?"*

- Allow participants to answer the question. (You may choose to write their comments on a flip chart.)

  ⇨ Facilitator Says: *"Now how are we going to take action and put our solution into motion?"*

- Allow participants to answer the question. (You may choose to write their comments on a flip chart.)

  ⇨ Facilitator Says: *"Great job today. Now we will wrap up with an activity that will allow us to reflect on what we have learned about problem solving."*

Exploring What We Learned Today

The following OPTIONS are designed (a) to provide participants with more reflection opportunities, (b) to provide facilitators with a method to assess learning, and (c) to provide additional opportunities for learning to be applied. Facilitators may choose to complete *one or more of the options* from the following list based on time available and the overall goals of your organization's leadership and environmental stewardship program.

- OPTION 1: Have each participant break down a problem facing him over the next day and identify the steps of the process he will use to solve it.

- OPTION 2: Divide into small groups and evaluate the effectiveness (or ineffectiveness) of your organization's recycling efforts. Questions to ponder: Are the hiking trails free of litter? Are there specific bins to throw away trash or recycled items? Are these bins conveniently located? Are the dining facilities utilizing reusable materials to serve or store food instead of using more consumable items? Participants should determine how the practices can be improved by utilizing the steps in the problem-solving process. Once improvements and possible solutions have been identified, share all ideas with the large group. The large group will then choose one or a combination of two or more ideas to implement during this program session.

- OPTION 3: Ask participants to answer the following questions (either aloud as a group or in their journals) by answering either "true" or "false" to each question.
  - ✓ A strategy is a plan of action intended to create a solution to a specific problem.
  - ✓ The first strategy in solving a problem is to establish criteria to evaluate solutions.
  - ✓ Problems are solved by working through the five strategies of the problem-solving process.
  - ✓ When analyzing a problem, examining what makes it a problem is important.
  - ✓ Every problem should have more than one solution. It is up to the individual to select the most beneficial solution.

- OPTION 4: Ask participants to read and think about the following scenario: As you and your family are parking the car at your local grocery store, you notice two large recycling Dumpsters sitting in the parking lot; one is for paper and one is for plastic and glass. You get out of the car, begin walking up to the front doors of the store, and notice that people leaving the grocery store are carrying their groceries in plastic bags. You walk into the store, get your cart, and pass the checkout lanes, only to see that the store does not offer paper or reusable bags to carry groceries out of the store. This concerns you because you have learned that plastics are made from such irreplaceable resources as crude oil, natural gas, and coal, and if not recycled properly, it can take hundreds of years before plastics can be broken down. As a small group, your task is to educate and encourage the store manager about ways to reduce, reuse, recycle, or possibly eliminate plastic usage when bagging groceries. Create a picture, flowchart, or mind map that outlines the solution to the problem.

Handout RR: Problem Solving Defined

Problem solving
is the
process
by which
problems are
identified
and solved.

Handout SS:
Six Steps of the
Problem-Solving Process

1. Identify the problem.

2. Collect all needed information.

3. Guess what the solution will be.

4. Test to see if your guess works.

5. See what the result is.

6. Retry until the wanted solution is reached.

Handout TT: Problem

INSTRUCTIONS: Cut the following lines into strips so participants can put them in the correct order.

Problem: Need summer job

Steps that need to be put in the correct order:

Receive a rejection letter with no interview.

Receive a job offer.

Look at job listings online and in a newspaper.

Prepare more thoroughly for the application and interview processes.

Complete a second job application and earn a job interview.

Complete a job application.

Handout UU:
Problem-Solving Strategies

What is a strategy?

- A strategy is a plan of action intended to create a solution to a specific problem.

Problem-solving strategies:

- Define the problem—what is the problem you want to solve?

- Analyze the problem—what makes this a problem?

- Establish criteria to evaluate solutions—how would I like to solve this problem?

- Propose solutions—what are the possible solutions?

- Take actions—what would be the best way to act on the solution I decided on?

Handout VV: Landfill Scenario

INSTRUCTIONS: Read the scenario below and follow the instructions.

The local landfill in your community is exhibiting some difficulties because of the amount of waste being produced in your community. The landfill was not expected to be at full capacity until the year 2025, but because of the excess waste that is being produced in the community, it is currently projected to be at full capacity within five years. One reason for the landfill filling quickly is the lack of an environmental stewardship program for the community. If such a plan were in place, this could help the community reduce, reuse, and recycle waste. One place that produces a lot of waste is your local school. Create possible solutions to help your school reduce, reuse, and recycle the waste produced by the student body. Utilize the five problem-solving strategies to help create possible solutions to this issue.

• Define the problem:

• Analyze the problem:

• Establish criteria to evaluate solutions:

• Propose solutions:

• Describe possible actions:

10

Identifying Resources

Learning Emphasis
- Define the term *resources.*
- Identify categories of resources and examples of each using environmental problems.
- Identify the benefits of asking for help and the types of individual and/or groups that can provide help.

Time Required
- 60–90 minutes (depending on number of activities completed)

Materials Needed
- Resource-related activities
- Pen/pencil for each participant
- Flip chart
- Matching cards (made from Handout AAA)
- Blank sheets of paper (one per participant)
- Participant journal (optional)
- Handouts WW through EEE

Activity Agenda
- Chapter Connection to Environmental Stewardship Project
- Rainy-Day Brainstorm Activity
- Recognizing Resources Activity
- My Knowledge and Skills Activity
- Artist–Talker Challenge Activity
- Asking for Help Activity
- Four-Way Nature Problem Activity
- Exploring What We Learned Today

Chapter Connection to Environmental Stewardship Project

⇨ Facilitator Says: *"In this portion of our leadership program, we will be learning how to identify community resources and to enlist support from others. Remember that we will all be challenged at the end of the program with leading an environmental project. Participants who are able to identify relevant resources and successfully seek out others to help with their projects will be better prepared and able to implement their environmental stewardship projects."*

Rainy-Day Brainstorm Activity

⇨ Facilitator Says: *"Rain is a fact of life. But what happens to scheduled programs when it rains? How do staff members (and we) have to respond? Let's say that an unexpected storm showed up right after lunch one day and it rained for five hours. What did the staff members do to keep participants actively involved and having fun? Specifically, what resources did the staff members need in order to keep the programs going?"*

- Have participants work with a partner to brainstorm a list of resources staff would use in this situation. Then, call on a few teams to share their lists.

Recognizing Resources Activity

⇨ Facilitator Says: *"Good job thinking through that scenario. So, what are 'resources'?"*

- Solicit feedback from the group.

⇨ Facilitator Says: *"Resources include all the information sources we use to solve problems. Raise your hand if you can think of times when you might need resources in your life."*

- Get several responses and then move on to categories of resources.

⇨ Facilitator Says: *"Now that we know the definition of resources, let's look at the three categories of resources."*

- Share Handout WW.

⇨ Facilitator Says: *"The three categories of resources are:*
✓ *Human resources—people who share knowledge or skills with you.*

✓ *Information resources—books, magazines, websites.*

✓ *Personal resources—something you know about or are talented at doing."*

• Have participants think of examples of each category and then write them in their journals.

⇨ Facilitator Says: *"In about one minute, identify at least two examples of a resource from each of the three categories."*

• Upon completion, ask several participants to share their answers.

⇨ Facilitator Says: *"You have done such a great job of identifying the three categories of resources! Now let's consider what makes those resources relevant. Using our three categories, think about what makes a resource the perfect fit for a solution or need. Therefore, we will now define what a relevant resource is."*

• Ask participants about "relevant" resources.

⇨ Facilitator Says: *"What is a relevant resource? Are all resources relevant? How would you determine if a resource was relevant for a particular problem you were trying to solve?"*

• Discuss participants' ideas and examples and then share Handout XX.

⇨ Facilitator Says: *"This handout shows how we define a relevant resources and offers some examples. So, let's think through resources that would be relevant for a specific environmental problem. I am going to give you a scenario and then divide you into three smaller groups. Each group will identify a list of relevant resources (human, information, and personal) to address the issue."*

• Divide the large group into three smaller groups. Each smaller group receives a copy of Handout YY. Ask participants to identify relevant resources related to each of the issues.

⇨ Facilitator Says (reading Handout YY): *"The U.S. government is encouraging every household to become environmental stewards. An area in which they are asking people to improve is the conservation of energy by establishing practices that will decrease the amount being used. If energy conservation is achieved, individual households will be rewarded with reduced energy costs, thereby promoting economic security. Create a list of energy-saving options that can be implemented in your household. Once the list is created, identify the types of resources you use to further explore each area so you can help your family reduce energy consumption and maximize cost savings. Try to think of examples of each category for your energy conservation project for your family. I will give you a few minutes to do this."*

• After ample time has passed, ask a few participants to share their examples.

⇨ Facilitator Says: *"You have done an excellent job of thinking about resources and how they apply to a specific problem. Now let's focus on the personal resources you bring to our group."*

My Knowledge and Skills Activity

⇨ Facilitator Says: *"Each of us brings special personal resources to our group and to the problems we try to solve. In order for each of us to respect the special resources that each of us bring to the table, take a few minutes to complete this personal resource inventory."*

• Pass out Handout ZZ and give participants two to three minutes to complete it. Once the participants complete the inventory, allow 30 seconds for them to share three of their personal resources with two neighbors either to their right or left.

⇨ Facilitator Says: *"The inventory each of you just completed is a reminder of the personal resources that you have available when trying to solve a problem. Now let's think about how to involve others to help us solve problems."*

Artist–Talker Challenge Activity

• This activity will help participants realize that when they are trying to solve problems, they may need another person or group to help them. As participants enter the room, hand each of them a word card. Every two participants will get the same word on their cards. Cards can be found on Handout AAA.

⇨ Facilitator Says: *"In front of us is a card with a word on it. I want you to find the person in the room who has the same word card as you. We will have 30 seconds to find our partner and sit together. Go!"*

• Wait 30 seconds and be sure everyone has a partner. The participants do not need to take anything with them.

⇨ Facilitator Says: *"Great job! The person next to us will be our partner for today. Now I want you to decide who in your partner team will be the artist and who will be the talker. Each group will receive a sheet of paper with a drawing on it, an overhead sheet, and a marker. You will have 15 seconds to decide."*

• Provide a few seconds for partners to determine their roles.

⇨ Facilitator Says: *"Who are my artists? The artists will draw a picture on the upper half of the overhead sheet with the marker while keeping their eyes closed! You may not ask any questions, and you must draw what the talker tells you to draw."*

⇨ Facilitator Says: *"As for my talkers, you will give directions to the artist on how to draw the picture. We will have three minutes to complete our work of art. Time* starts when everyone receives the paper. Remember, artists, keep your eyes closed, and please do not talk or ask questions."

- Distribute one copy of Handout BBB to each artist.

  ⇨ Facilitator Says: *"You may begin!"*

- Allow time for participants to create their artwork.

  ⇨ Facilitator Says: *"5 … 4 … 3 … 2 … 1 … Time is up! Put your markers down. Wonderful! I saw some really good things happening in the group during our drawing session. So, let's talk about what you experienced."*

- Allow partner groups the opportunity to share their pictures with the entire group and to describe what they were thinking and feeling during the activity.

  ⇨ Facilitator Says: *"What made it difficult to solve this problem? Why?"*

- Solicit feedback from participants.

  ⇨ Facilitator Says: *"What would have made it easier to solve the problem? Why?"*

- Solicit feedback from participants.

  ⇨ Facilitator Says: *"One of the keys to success with this activity was clear communication. Particularly when we are asking others for help, communication can sometimes be difficult, especially if two people have a different vision for what the solution to the problem might be."*

  ⇨ Facilitator Says: *"It would have been very difficult if I had told you to close your eyes and draw the picture without the assistance of your partner. Many times, we face problems in our lives we are unable to solve by ourselves. We may need to ask for help. So, today, we will discover the benefits of asking for help in developing solutions to problems. Let's also identify individuals whom we should ask to help us. In order for us to discover these exciting ideas, we will need to be willing to admit we cannot do everything on our own. This involves taking a risk, but together, we will be successful!"*

Asking for Help Activity

⇨ Facilitator Says (referring to Handout CCC): *"Let's capture our answers to the following questions in our journals:*
  ✓ *When should someone seek assistance in solving a problem?*
  ✓ *What type of individual or groups of people should someone ask for help?*
  ✓ *What benefits do you think a person can receive in asking for help?*

You will have four minutes to answer these questions."

- Wait four minutes and then discuss participants' answers to these questions. You may choose to capture the answers on a flip chart.

  ⇨ Facilitator Says: *"Look at the variety of answers! It is important for people to seek out others for assistance when solving problems. Keep the following in mind when seeking out people for help."*

  ⇨ Facilitator Says (referring to Handout DDD): *"The benefits of asking for help can include:*
  ✓ *Sharing the load of the problem*
  ✓ *Getting more possible solutions*
  ✓ *Drawing on someone else's strengths and experiences*
  ✓ *Getting more support and guidance for solving the problem"*

  ⇨ Facilitator Says (still referring to Handout DDD): *"And as many of you shared, we can ask lots of different people to be resources for us and to help us solve problems, including parents and family, friends, facilitators and guidance counselors, community leaders, clergy, and public service people. Who are we leaving out? Is there anyone we should add to this list?"*

Four-Way Nature Problem Activity

  ⇨ Facilitator Says: *"We have now learned the benefits of asking for help and have identified people to help us with our problem solving. Now we can apply what we have learned to nature-based problems."*

- Using the four scenarios outlined on Handout EEE, split participants into four teams and assign one scenario to each team. Allow each team enough time to brainstorm a list of people who could potentially help with the issue. After ample time has passed, encourage each team to share its scenario and list of others to help with the issue with the entire group. (Note: You may choose to create new or modify existing scenarios to be more specific to your organization.)

  ⇨ Facilitator Says: *"In this activity, you will select a partner and choose a scenario from the list provided in Handout EEE. Participants will brainstorm a list of people who could potentially help with the issue stated in their specific scenario. Be prepared to share your scenario and list with the group. Discuss how these individuals and others not mentioned could be of service to finding a solution for the problem."*

- Give each group ample time to discuss its scenario. Allow groups to report back regarding the lists of resources they developed.

  ⇨ Facilitator Says: *"Today, we were able to examine how important it is to ask for help when faced with problems that need solving. Many times, asking for help will allow us to explore many different solutions. Many of these solutions may be ones that we may not have achieved on our own. Sometimes, we might need to share the problem with someone and get help so we can make a wise decision. Never be afraid to share the problems we are having with someone. If we do not ask for help when we need it, we will never know the potential a person may have to help us solve your problems."*

Exploring What We Learned Today

The following OPTIONS are designed (a) to provide participants with more reflection opportunities, (b) to provide facilitators with a method to assess learning, and (c) to provide additional opportunities for learning to be applied. Facilitators may choose to complete *one or more of the options* from the following list based on time available and the overall goals of your organization's leadership and environmental stewardship program.

- OPTION 1: Ask each participant to read and think about the following scenario: As a society, we rely heavily on wireless technology for our communications. According to research from Wireless Intelligence, the number of global mobile connections surpassed the 5 billion mark in 2010 and the average wireless phone subscriber exchanges, upgrades, or obtains a new phone every 18 months, which, according to the U.S. Environmental Protection Agency, equals more than 130 million cell phones discarded annually. This in turn creates an estimated 65,000 tons of electronic garbage. Brainstorm potential solutions to help reduce the amount of electronic garbage that is being discarded each year. Participants should select one possible solution and identify the possible resources they can use to gain additional information to strengthen their solution. Next, participants should work in groups of three to research their solution and create an infomercial to present to the large group.

- OPTION 2: Ask participants to answer the following questions (either aloud as a group or in their journals) by answering either "true" or "false" to each question.
   - ✓ A resource is a collective wealth of knowledge critical to solving problems.
   - ✓ You should never ask for assistance when trying to solve a problem.
   - ✓ The three categories of resources are human, personal, and index.
   - ✓ Parents are not a source you should consult when seeking a solution to a problem.
   - ✓ Relevant resources are those that are logically related to the problem at hand.
   - ✓ An example of an information resource is a website.
   - ✓ Some benefits to asking for help are the sharing of the weight of the problem and getting support.

- OPTION 3: Select an environmental issue that is very important and relevant to your organization or to the participants. In pairs, have participants write at least one example of the following resources related to the selected issue: human, information, and personal. Have participants work to collect the appropriate resources on the topic of choice. Then, allow participants an opportunity to craft a song or chant that incorporates their research and expresses the important information about the environmental issue.

- OPTION 4: Place participants in groups based on the types of environmental projects they might be interested in addressing. Instruct them to think through the types of resources they will need and the people they can ask to help them with their projects. They can capture their thinking in their journals or report back to the overall group.

Handout WW:
Categories of Resources

- Human resources—individuals who have knowledge and skills that are willing to share information with you

- Information resources—books, magazines, websites, etc.

- Personal resources—something you know about or are talented at doing

Handout XX:
Relevant Resources

"Relevant resources" → those logically related to the problem you are trying to solve

• Relevant human resources

✓ Examples include friends, teachers, counselors, or principals in school; people from a church or place of spiritual growth; boss or coworkers; parents or their friends; your friends

• Relevant information resources

✓ Examples include Internet, library, school books, magazines

• Relevant personal resources

✓ Examples include talents or capabilities you have, such as singing, speaking, sports, good grades

Handout YY: Energy Steward Exercise

The U.S. government is encouraging every household to become environmental stewards. An area in which they are asking people to improve is the conservation of energy by establishing practices that will decrease the amount being used. If energy conservation is achieved, individual households will be rewarded with reduced energy costs, thereby promoting economic security. Create a list of energy-saving options that can be implemented in your household. Once the list is created, identify the types of resources you use to further explore each area so you can help your family reduce energy consumption and maximize cost savings.

Handout ZZ: Personal Resource Inventory

INSTRUCTIONS: Using the following list, put a check mark (✓) next to the personal resource items you consider yourself to be good at.

_____ Singing

_____ Playing sports

_____ Computer programming

_____ Playing an instrument

_____ Working with people

_____ Reading

_____ Writing

_____ Performing in a play

_____ Electronic gaming

_____ Public speaking

_____ Drawing

_____ Team competitions

_____ Memorizing facts

_____ Debating

_____ Mentoring others

_____ Working with children

_____ Managing money

_____ Other items not on this list

1. _____

2. _____

3. _____

4. _____

Handout AAA:
Matching Pairs for Artist–Talker Activity

Facilitator	Facilitator
Computer programmer	Computer programmer
Counselor	Counselor
Principal	Principal
Parent	Parent
Police Officer	Police Officer
Firefighter	Firefighter
Doctor	Doctor
Nurse	Nurse
Leader	Leader
Friend	Friend
Family	Family
Problem	Problem
Help	Help
Sister	Sister
Brother	Brother
Clergy	Clergy
Specialist	Specialist
Scientist	Scientist
Solution	Solution
Adult	Adult

Handout BBB: Picture for Artist–Talker Activity

INSTRUCTIONS: Participants will sketch this picture on a piece of paper. One person in the group (the artist) will close his eyes while his partner (the talker) describes the picture that is to be drawn.

Handout CCC:
Questions Related to
Asking for Help

• When should someone seek assistance in solving a problem?

• What type of people or groups of people should someone ask for help?

• What benefits do you think a person can receive by asking for help?

Handout DDD:
Seeking Help From Others

Benefits of Seeking Help From Others

• To share the load of the problem

• To get more possible solutions

• To draw on someone else's strengths and experiences

• To provide support

• To give guidance

Individuals/Groups That Can Help

• Parents and family

• Friends

• Facilitators and guidance counselors

• Service people: police, community leaders, clergy

• Community leaders

• Anyone who may benefit you in solving your problem

Handout EEE:
Exploring Resources for
Nature-Based Problems

INSTRUCTIONS: Select a partner and choose a scenario from the list below. Participants will brainstorm a list of people who could potentially help with the issue stated in their specific scenario. Be prepared to share your scenario and list with the group. Discuss how these individuals and others not mentioned could be of service to finding a solution for the problem.

• Water conservation is the most cost-effective and environmentally sound way to reduce our demand for water. The camp would like to start a water conservation program to help reduce costs and the environmental impact. What types of individuals or groups should you ask for help when brainstorming ideas or developing a water conservation programs?

• The camp has decided to start a recycling program to help reduce the amount of waste being taken to landfills. What types of individuals or groups should you ask for help when trying to determine the kinds of materials that are accepted for recycling in your area?

• The nature center at the camp is going to be closed due to lack of funding. What types of individuals or groups should you ask for help in brainstorming ideas and implementing a plan of action for keeping the nature center open?

• The neighborhood has decided to start a community garden. Community gardens provide individuals access to fresh produce as well as a sense of community and connection to the environment. The organizing committee, of which you are a member, has decided to find a sponsor—an individual or organization—to support the community garden. What types of individuals or groups should you ask for sponsorship to help with the community garden?

11

Facilitating Environmental Stewardship Projects

Learning Emphasis
- Design an action plan for environmental stewardship.
- Understand community resources for environmental stewardship.

Time Required
- 30–60 minutes (depending on number of activities completed)

Materials Needed
- Project-related activities
- Pen/pencil for each participant
- Participant journal (optional)
- Handouts FFF and GGG
- Access to community leaders (in person, by phone, Skype, etc.) (optional)

Activity Agenda
- Chapter Connection to Environmental Stewardship Project
- Designing My Personal Environmental Stewardship Action Plan Activity
- Involving Community Leaders Activity

Chapter Connection to Environmental Stewardship Project

- The foundation for environmental stewardship has been built. Participants have learned important information about leadership, character, teamwork, building relationships, taking initiative, goal setting, problem solving, and identifying resources. They have also applied what they have learned to a number of environmental and nature-based problems. Some participants may have even identified an environmental issue or problem around which they have started to identify goals, the steps for solving the problem, and what they would need to address the issue. Now is the time when the knowledge and skills that participants have learned will be integrated into the creation of a take-home environmental stewardship action plan (ESAP), which allows participants to outline how they will address an environmental problem or issue in their camps, homes, schools, or communities.

Designing My Personal Environmental Stewardship Action Plan Activity

⇨ Facilitator Says: *"Remember that the goal of our program was to learn about leadership so we would be prepared for service after the end of this program. Now it is time for us to combine what we have learned about leadership and solving nature-based problems into a plan. This is your environmental stewardship action plan, and it might look very different from the plan of the person on your right or your left. That is because the nature-based problems that impact you or that are important to you may be different from the issues that are important to others."*

- Distribute Handout FFF.

⇨ Facilitator Says: *"Feel free to be creative and to start from scratch or to build on an idea you have started during the course of this leadership program. You have already been thinking about setting environmental goals and solving nature-based problems, so if you have an idea for an environmental stewardship project, then that is great. Go ahead and build on your idea to complete your action plan. On the other hand, if you have not decided what problem you want to focus on for your project, you can take this time to come up with a new idea."*

- You may choose to distribute Handout GGG or simply share some of the ideas with participants who are struggling to think of a project idea.

⇨ Facilitator Says: *"Thinking about your resources is really important. It is easy to think of an idea today while we are all together, but it is another thing to actually be able to take action when each of us returns home. Who can help you with your project? What local groups might be able to help or provide you with information?"*

• After participants have completed their plans, have them come together in small groups based on the environmental problem they hope to address. Ask them to share their plans with the other participants in their small group. What can they learn from each other? Are there opportunities to share resources or even work together? (This might be an option if participants live near one another, which might be true for some of your participants.)

Involving Community Leaders Activity

⇨ Facilitator Says: *"When you were creating your plan, many of you probably identified people in your community who could be resources. Several community leaders are with us today to learn about your projects and to share their knowledge and expertise with us. I am pleased to welcome…"*

• See Appendix D for community resources you might want to share with participants. If you have scheduled local community leaders to visit your program, this would be the perfect opportunity to integrate their involvement. Have participants present their ideas to the community leaders for feedback or ideas on how to get started, who to contact for support, etc.

Handout FFF: Personal Environmental Stewardship Action Plan

Name: _____

1. The problem that my project will address is:

2. The goal of my project will be to:

3. I will start my project on (or around) this date:

4. To complete my project, I will have to take the following steps:

5. Resources I will need to complete my project include (human, information, and/or personal):

6. Potential obstacles to the completion of my project include:

7. I will know my project is a success if/when:

Handout GGG:
Environmental Stewardship Project Ideas

- Start a home recycling program. You might focus on the type of items family members will agree to recycle (newspaper, plastic, aluminum, clear glass, colored glass).
- Grow a home garden. Integrate homegrown vegetables into meals or flowers/plants into landscaping.
- Mentor or teach local elementary school children about conservation (do not waste water, switch to compact fluorescent lightbulbs, etc.).
- Create a neighborhood hiking club.
- Plant flowers in a community park.
- Start a recycling program.
- Assist older adults in your community with landscape/garden projects.
- Teach local elementary school children about the importance of nature.
- Start a community cell phone recycling program.
- Start a school (or classroom) cell phone recycling program.
- Build a nature trail in your neighborhood.
- Plant trees at your school or in your neighborhood/community.
- Offer to read aloud to children younger than you. Select nature-related books.
- Start a neighborhood birding club and/or wildlife club.
- Adopt a community park (keep the park litter-free, weed the flowerbeds, plant some flowers).
- Teach your schoolmates to reduce the amount of food waste, and encourage the school kitchen to donate leftover food to a local food bank or farmers.
- Plan an Earth Day event in your neighborhood. Earth Day is celebrated around the world on April 22. Some cities start celebrating a week in advance, ending the recognition of Earth Week on April 22. Others host month-long events.
- Write letters (start a campaign) to local legislators about the importance of protecting the environment.
- Encourage friends to carry a water bottle rather than paper cups or running a fountain.
- Adopt a stream, lake, or another waterway at your site or in your community.
- Generate lists of ways to do things with less water. Create posters to share ideas with your organization, your community, your school community, or your neighborhood.
- Write a book (or poems) for younger children about ways to protect the environment.
- Use recycled paper products.
- Teach schoolmates to take their lunch to school in reusable containers, and encourage your school to use real dishes and silverware.

12

Evaluating the Outcomes of Youth Leadership and Environmental Stewardship

Youth Program Evaluation and Intentionality

Youth program providers using this book are encouraged to evaluate the outcomes or benefits that youth receive through participation in a camp-based leadership and environmental stewardship program. While evaluation has long been connected with programs at many camps, the majority of camps have historically focused on measuring youth and parent satisfaction with the program rather than how well the program met its goals (Henderson, Bialeschki, & James, 2007). Satisfaction measures—such as "How well did you enjoy camp?"—necessarily emphasize "outputs" (i.e., the results of a programming effort and participants' reactions to the program) versus "outcomes" (i.e., changes in learning, behaviors, or conditions). Over the past decade, outcome-focused evaluation approaches have become more commonplace in camps, with some guided by logic modeling, and these approaches have improved the capacity of camps and other organizations to document program impacts (Arnold, 2006). This outcome-focused evaluation has allowed a progression of thinking from happenstance to intentionality (Garst, 2010).

In the past, many camps have been forced to use outcomes measures that were either untested or not specific to the camp setting (Garst, 2010). For example, camps have used self-esteem measures designed for school settings to measure how camp influences a child's sense of self. Over the past few years, new resources have emerged to meet the increased expectations from funding agencies administrators who want systematic outcome evaluation documentation and even logic models that reflect intentional programming and evidence-based practices (Bialeschki & Conn, 2011). Camp-specific resources, such as the ACA's Youth Outcomes Battery (2009), have been developed to support an outcome-focused approach.

The impact of the camp experience on the development of leadership and life skills among older youth and counselors has been the focus of numerous studies (DeGraaf & Glover, 2003; James, 2003; Lyons, 2000; Powell, Bixler, & Switzer, 2003; Forsythe,

Matysik, & Nelson; 2004; Garst & Johnson, 2005; Toupence & Townsend, 2000). One of the few studies that examined camp-based leadership and environmental stewardship outcomes was the two-year California 4-H Camp Study (Bird et al., 2008). Very little research has examined the outcomes associated with specific leadership curricula used in camp leadership training programs. In 2009 and 2010, the American Camp Association evaluated the outcomes of the Camp 2 Grow leadership and environmental stewardship program on the enhancement of knowledge and skills in these areas (Garst, Bialeschki, & Browne, 2010).

Camp 2 Grow Evaluation Model

Using the Camp 2 Grow Evaluation Model

This section outlines the evaluation model that was used with the ACA's Camp 2 Grow program (Garst, Bialeschki, & Browne, 2010). Because this model proved effective for measuring the youth outcomes associated with the leadership and environmental stewardship curriculum presented in this book, program providers using this book may want to use a similar evaluation model based on the study design, instrumentation, and evaluation steps utilized for Camp 2 Grow.

Study Design

A mixed-methods evaluation plan was designed to assess the effectiveness of Camp 2 Grow in fostering environmental stewardship among summer camp participants (Browne, Garst, & Bialeschki, 2011). A purposive sample consisting of 24 day and resident camps was selected to participate in the study based on geographic region, population and the number of participants served, agency affiliation, and nature program focus. Data were collected from participants by using a self-report survey and from parents and camp staff by using an online SurveyMonkey survey. Repeated measures analysis was used to assess the impact of time spent at a nature-based camp that included the Camp 2 Grow curriculum on measures of participants' perceived leadership skills, affinity for nature, and sense of empowerment.

Independence, problem solving, affinity for nature, and empowerment showed significant gains over time (from pretest to posttest) after adjusting for multiple comparisons. Results of this study indicated that time spent at a nature-based camp that includes the Camp 2 Grow program effectively fosters many of the facets that contribute to environmental stewardship. Specifically, Camp 2 Grow participants demonstrated gains in independence, problem solving, affinity for nature, and empowerment.

Evaluation Plan Components

Evaluation Logic Model

A logic model was designed to illustrate the goals, inputs, and outcomes for Camp 2 Grow. This model was a framework for the evaluation plan (Figure 12-1).

Concepts Measured

The evaluation plan was designed to assess growth in the following leadership and environmental stewardship areas:

- Leadership outcomes (teamwork, social problem solving/decision making, responsibility, independence, civic engagement, empowerment)
- Nature affinity and stewardship outcomes (emotional affinity for nature, stewardship behaviors)
- Youths' intention to act (to complete their environmental stewardship action plans)

Goals	Inputs	Outputs	Short-Term Outcomes	Long-Term Outcomes
Leadership knowledge and skills Environmental stewardship knowledge and skills	Youth who are participating in the program Staff who are trained to lead the program Leadership curriculum: • Teamwork • Leadership • Building positive relationships • Service, citizenship, and community • Character • Taking risks • Problem solving • Planning	Number of youth who completed the program Number of staff who were engaged as facilitators of the program Number of environmental stewardship projects completed	Increased leadership attitudes and behaviors: • Teamwork • Responsibility • Independence • Problem solving • Confidence Increased beliefs about stewardship Emotional affinity for nature Increased feelings of empowerment	Youth are community leaders. Youth are practicing environmental stewardship. Communities improve through youth engagement.

Figure 12-1. Camp 2 Grow program evaluation logic model

Instrumentation

Youth Survey

A 36-item youth self-report survey—used for the pretest and posttest (see Appendices B and C)—was compiled from six scales designed to assess participants' growth in the domains identified as part of environmental leadership (i.e., affinity for nature, teamwork, responsibility, independence, empowerment, and problem solving). Each of these areas was captured by a scale adapted from the ACA Youth Outcomes Battery (Ellis, Sibthorp, & Bialeschki, 2007; Sibthorp, 2008), except for empowerment, which was constructed from three items from the Characteristics of the Experience Scale (Sibthorp, 2001). Each of the items from these scales was measured along a six-point Likert scale in which responses ranged from 1 (false) to 6 (true). The youth survey was administered on the first day of camp. In addition to measuring gains in specified outcomes related to leadership and connection to nature from pretest to posttest, the survey also measured participants' follow-through on intentions established at camp to design and implement an environmental stewardship project upon their return from camp.

Participant Journal

Participants completed journaling throughout the Camp 2 Grow program, in much the same way as participants are encouraged to journal through the activities presented in Chapters 2 through 11 in this book. The journals included such guiding questions as:
- How will you use your new knowledge and skills to benefit your family, neighborhood, school, or community?
- If you could teach your friends one thing that you learned in the Camp 2 Grow leadership training program at camp, what would it be?
- Being at camp has influenced the way I think about nature and being outdoors by...

Parent Survey

The parents of selected participants were asked to complete an online SurveyMonkey survey approximately four to six weeks following the end of the session in which their children participated in Camp 2 Grow (Appendix D). The survey was designed to assess parents' perceptions of their children since they returned from camp. Questions focused on aspects of environmental leadership, the environmental stewardship project planned by the children, and parent demographic information. The survey targeted leadership behaviors and expressions of connections to nature that were associated with involvement in Camp 2 Grow.

Staff Survey

Camp 2 Grow staff and directors were asked to complete a survey similar to the parent survey at the end of the camp session during which Camp2Grow was implemented (Appendix E). Staff provided their perceptions about participants' environmental leadership knowledge and skills as well as an assessment of the curriculum lessons.

Key Evaluation Findings and Conclusions

The following key findings (American Camp Association, 2011a) summarize the results of the ACA's evaluation of Camp 2 Grow:

- The C2G curriculum was effective in bringing about increased leadership (as defined by characteristics of independence, citizenship, and problem solving), environmental stewardship, and an overall sense of empowerment among youth participants.

- Campers expressed that their new knowledge and skills would benefit their family, schools, and communities by instilling in them a willingness to help others, become engaged in environmental efforts, and improve their individual abilities (i.e., respectful, responsible, organized).

- Campers felt that C2G helped them learn important aspects about themselves, such as how to become a good leader and role model, improve personal attributes (maturity, patience, and mindfulness), how to work with others, and how to set goals and work hard to meet them.

- Campers indicated that being at camp influenced the way they thought about nature and the outdoors by increasing their appreciation and enjoyment of nature, learning respect for all living things, encouraging them to simplify and take a break from technology, lessening their fears, and just having fun in the outdoors.

- Camp staff indicated that upon completion of the C2G curriculum, their campers were more accepting of leadership roles, more of a team player, independent, confident, and more likely to think through solutions to problems before taking action.

- Parents indicated that upon returning home from camp, their C2G camper seemed more independent, more comfortable in the outdoors, more connected to the natural environment, more likely to talk positively about their leadership, and more likely to take actions that support their beliefs.

Youth Program Evaluation Tips

Based on lessons learned from the Camp2Grow program and other national evaluation projects, the following are several tips to keep in mind when planning and implementing a youth program evaluation:

- Engage staff in the program evaluation process to encourage buy-in, to better understand what is important to them, and to model your organization's commitment to quality programming.

- Create a logic model for your program (i.e., goals, inputs, outputs, and outcomes), and determine how you will measure success.

- Be clear in the design and implementation steps to have concrete, measurable targets that focus the evaluation,

- Determine what questions will be asked to evaluate the program goals you outlined in your logic model and the best ways to collect data to answer your questions. Will you collect information from youth, parents, staff, or some combination of these groups?

- Inform stakeholders of your program evaluation plans. If you will be collecting information from them (for example, from parents and caregivers), help them understand their role in the evaluation process and how you will use the feedback they provide.

- Use consistent data collection techniques and tools (for example, the same instruments).

- Use measurement tools that are reliable and valid. Also, try to find measurement tools that have been tested and used with youth similar to those involved in the program you are evaluating.

- If you plan to collect data across multiple years, be prepared to ask the same (or similar) questions over time so you can compare results in a meaningful way.

- Train your staff in the evaluation process and their roles in the process.

- Secure adequate support and resources to carry out the evaluation. You may need people to enter data, to facilitate focus groups, to transcribe interviews, etc.

- Consider reaching out to local colleges and universities for program evaluation support. Undergraduate and graduate students are often looking for projects, and they might be a critical resource for your organization.

- Write a brief summary report that can serve as a benchmark for your program, particularly for multiyear programs.

- Understand that it is okay to have results that may not all be positive. You will likely find that such data are the most helpful for making appropriate program improvement decisions.

- When your program evaluation results become available, report the results to organizational stakeholders (such as administration, staff, program participants, funders, donors, and alumni).

- Tell your story. Think about how your results might be shared via local media, your website, your social media strategies, etc.

- Most importantly, do not allow program evaluation results to sit on a shelf. Schedule time to review program evaluation results with the appropriate administrative and programmatic staff within your organization. Explore the implications of the results. Use the results to inform program and/or organizational improvements.

- If programs are improved or changed because of the input you received from youth, staff, parents, or another group, tell them about the changes and thank them again for their involvement in the evaluation process.

13

Reflections on Nature, Leadership, and Stewardship

We trust that you have enjoyed this exploration of youth leadership and environmental stewardship guided and informed by the ACA's Camp 2 Grow program. More importantly, we hope that the concepts and ideas taught by the activities in this book helped your youth participants think more deeply about their roles as leaders in solving nature-based problems.

Camp will always be a powerful setting for exposing children to nature and teaching youth about leadership and environmental stewardship. Opportunities to learn and practice leadership are engrained in the camp experience, but at some camps, these opportunities are presented to campers in subtle ways to avoid the perception that camp is too much like school (Garst & Chavez, 2010). The argument for subtlety is sometimes phrased as "We teach kids without them realizing that they are learning," like blending spinach in a smoothie to mask the fact that the drink contains green vegetables. Unfortunately, the subtle approach can lead to happenstance (some youth will "get it" and some will not) or a failure of youth and parents to attribute positive outcomes to the impact of your programs. Explicitly labeling leadership, modeling leadership and environmental stewardship, and providing opportunities for youth to practice leadership allow program providers to avoid the pitfalls of happenstance. Structured curricula, such as the one presented in this book, offer an effective approach for targeting desired youth outcomes (Browne, Garst, & Bialeschki, 2011). When combined with opportunities to spend meaningful time in nature, to engage in critical thinking around nature-based problem solving, and to take action to solve relevant environmental issues, leadership skill-building activities can develop a young person's identity as an environmental steward.

How often do we as youth development professionals provide youth with opportunities for community-based service and stewardship? It has been noted that "engaged citizens do not create themselves. We should no more expect spontaneous engagement than we do spontaneous combustion. The norms of the culture are against the former, just as the laws of physics are against the latter" (Keeter et al., 2002, p. 2). In some youth programs, instead of legitimate involvement, voice, and control, youth may be given token positions or leadership under tight direction from adults. An important feature of the curriculum highlighted in this book is the active engagement of youth in important community issues. Youth engagement is a critical aspect of positive youth development (Benson & Pittman, 2001; Yohalem & Martin, 2007), and opportunities for youth to participate alongside adults present benefits to youth and to the community (Browne, Garst, & Bialeschki, 2011). Perhaps the greatest catalyst for engaging youth in community-based service and leadership through this book is the connections that are encouraged between young people and community leaders in the planning for the environmental stewardship action plans. What results emerged at your camp (or in your organization) when young people and community representatives came together to discuss local environmental problems? If community representatives were not invited to be involved when you implemented this curriculum, consider how you might reach out and involve them in the future.

Youth engagement with nature as the conduit is easier than it may seem. Sure, some children and teenagers are like fish out of water when in an outdoor setting. Because youth often spend much of their time indoors and in front of some form of electronic medium, nature seems quite foreign to them. But experiencing nature at camp—and through other informal youth programs—is a unique undertaking. Where else can young people gaze at the stars, feel a stream bubble between their toes, or watch a campfire—all while being surrounded by caring peers and adults in a setting that has a duration and intensity beyond what most children and teenagers get to experience in other places and spaces. At a time when a significant concern exists about the lack of meaningful contact that many children have with nature and an urgency to provide resources to re-engage youth and families in nature-based experiences, we see history repeating itself as the importance of camp experiences is reiterated. In the 1910s, the popular press recognized campers' love of the outdoors and documented the learning opportunities that summer camps offered (Ozier, 2010). Vinal (1935) noted that in the early 19th century, the "shortage of fresh air that [was] the result of herding in large cities" resulted in a "return to the soil, the forests, and the lakes" and that "summer camp was one phase of this back-to-the-country movement" (p. 16). Now is the time to leverage the power, novelty, and meanings of nature to fully engage young people—to be purposeful in our efforts to create tomorrow's leaders and environmental stewards today.

Appendix A:
Summary of Handouts

- Chapter 2: Leadership
  - ✓ Handout A: Leadership Characteristics Tree
  - ✓ Handout B: Terms Associated With Leadership
  - ✓ Handout C: Definition of Leadership
  - ✓ Handout D: Who Are the Leaders
  - ✓ Handout E: Defining Leadership Styles
  - ✓ Handout F: Leadership Style Inventory
  - ✓ Handout G: Identifying Types of Leadership Styles
  - ✓ Handout H: Strengths and Challenges of Each Leadership Style

- Chapter 3: Character
  - ✓ Handout I: Defining Values, Beliefs, Character, and Integrity
  - ✓ Handout J: How Values, Beliefs, Character, and Integrity Benefit Leaders
  - ✓ Handout K: Scenarios for "Scenario Cards Activity"
  - ✓ Handout L: Examples of Responsibility and Accountability
  - ✓ Handout M: Participant Interview Guide: Values, Beliefs, Character, and Integrity

- Chapter 4: Teamwork
  - ✓ Handout N: Our Organizational Groups
  - ✓ Handout O: Groups vs. Teams
  - ✓ Handout P: How to Tell the Difference Between a Group and a Team
  - ✓ Handout Q: Benefits of Teamwork
  - ✓ Handout R: Leader Roles in a Team Activity
  - ✓ Handout S: Qualities a Leader Should Look for in Team Members
  - ✓ Handout T: My Leadership Assessment

- Chapter 5: Building Positive Relationships
  - ✓ Handout U: I Know!
  - ✓ Handout V: Attitude Observation
  - ✓ Handout W: Ways to Boost Attitudes as a Leader

- ✓ Handout X: Bartering Cards
- ✓ Handout Y: Ways to Build a Relationship
- ✓ Handout Z: Ideas for Strengthening a Relationship

- Chapter 6: Service
  - ✓ Handout AA: What Is Service?
  - ✓ Handout BB: Quotations on the Benefits of Service
  - ✓ Handout CC: What Are Needs?
  - ✓ Handout DD: Needs in My Camp, Family, School, and Community
  - ✓ Handout EE: Opportunities for Service Grid
  - ✓ Handout FF: My Service Activity
  - ✓ Handout GG: Coupon for My Service Activity

- Chapter 7: Taking Initiative
  - ✓ Handout HH: Qualities of a Self-Starter
  - ✓ Handout II: Qualities of Being Independent
  - ✓ Handout JJ: How Well Do You Work Independently?

- Chapter 8: Setting and Achieving Goals
  - ✓ Handout KK: S.M.A.R.T. Environmental Goals
  - ✓ Handout LL: Setting an Environmental S.M.A.R.T. Goal
  - ✓ Handout MM: Why Goals Fail
  - ✓ Handout NN: Goal-Related Quotes
  - ✓ Handout OO: Parts of a Goal-Setting Plan
  - ✓ Handout PP: Example of a Completed Goal-Setting Plan
  - ✓ Handout QQ: My Goal-Setting Plan

- Chapter 9: Problem Solving and Planning
  - ✓ Handout RR: Problem Solving Defined
  - ✓ Handout SS: Six Steps of the Problem-Solving Process
  - ✓ Handout TT: Problem
  - ✓ Handout UU: Problem-Solving Strategies
  - ✓ Handout VV: Landfill Scenario

- Chapter 10: Identifying Resources
  - ✓ Handout WW: Categories of Resources
  - ✓ Handout XX: Relevant Resources
  - ✓ Handout YY: Energy Steward Exercise
  - ✓ Handout ZZ: Personal Resource Inventory
  - ✓ Handout AAA: Matching Pairs for Artist–Talker Activity
  - ✓ Handout BBB: Picture for Artist–Talker Activity
  - ✓ Handout CCC: Questions Related to Asking for Help
  - ✓ Handout DDD: Seeking Help From Others
  - ✓ Handout EEE: Exploring Resources for Nature-Based Problems

- Chapter 11: Facilitating Environmental Stewardship Projects
  - ✓ Handout FFF: Personal Environmental Stewardship Action Plan
  - ✓ Handout GGG: Environmental Stewardship Project Ideas

Appendix B:
Camp 2 Grow Youth Survey
(Pretest)

american CAMP association®

© American Camp Association 2011

CAMP 2 GROW STARTING POINT QUESTIONS

**PLEASE READ THE INSTRUCTIONS BELOW BEFORE
TURNING THE PAGE AND BEGINNING THE SURVEY.**

This survey will ask you about your experiences *before coming to camp.* Please take a moment to examine the sample questions below.

Please look at sample question A) below. The camper filling out this survey believes that the phrase "I enjoy playing team sports" is *somewhat true* for him and checks "Somewhat True."

	False	Somewhat False	A Little True	Somewhat True	Mostly True	True
A) I enjoy playing team sports.	○	○	○	✓	○	○

Let's look at one more example before we start. For question B) below, the camper indicated that the statement "I enjoy being outdoors" is *a little true* and checks "A Little True."

	False	Somewhat False	A Little True	Somewhat True	Mostly True	True
B) I enjoy being outdoors.	○	○	✓	○	○	○

As you begin, please think carefully about each of your answers. It is very important to be accurate. No answers are right or wrong, and everyone will have different answers. Please put down what you actually think for each question.

Do you understand the instructions? **If no, please ask for help.** If yes, turn the page and begin.

Your responses are important and will help us make camp better for future campers!

Camp 2 Grow Youth Survey (Pretest) (cont.)

For the following set of questions, think about how you are when you are in your home or community.

	False	Somewhat False	A Little True	Somewhat True	Mostly True	True
1. I like being in nature.	O	O	O	O	O	O
2. I want to spend time outdoors.	O	O	O	O	O	O
3. I enjoy the freedom of being outside.	O	O	O	O	O	O
4. I am comfortable in the outdoors.	O	O	O	O	O	O
5. I feel connected to the natural environment.	O	O	O	O	O	O

(AFN-Pre)

For the following set of questions, think about the activities you do when you are at home, such as school, church, or community activities. Before each question, think to yourself, "At home, when I am participating in a group as a part of school or extracurricular activities…"

	False	Somewhat False	A Little True	Somewhat True	Mostly True	True
6. … I can help my group be successful.	O	O	O	O	O	O
7. … I can help others succeed.	O	O	O	O	O	O
8. … I can support my group members even when they have decided to do something I do not want to do.	O	O	O	O	O	O
9. … I can appreciate opinions that are different from my own.	O	O	O	O	O	O
10. … I can place group goals above the things I want.	O	O	O	O	O	O
11. … I can cooperate with others.	O	O	O	O	O	O
12. … I can be helpful in a small group of kids my age.	O	O	O	O	O	O
13. … I can work well with other people in a small group.	O	O	O	O	O	O
14. … I need less help from adults.	O	O	O	O	O	O
15. … I can make decisions by myself.	O	O	O	O	O	O
16. … I can make decisions without adults helping me .	O	O	O	O	O	O
17. … I can take care of myself.	O	O	O	O	O	O

Camp 2 Grow Youth Survey (Pretest) (cont.)

	False	Somewhat False	A Little True	Somewhat True	Mostly True	True
18. ... I accept responsibility for my actions.	○	○	○	○	○	○
19. ... I own up to my mistakes.	○	○	○	○	○	○
20. ... I do not blame others for my mistakes.	○	○	○	○	○	○
21. ... I try to make things right if I mess something up.	○	○	○	○	○	○
22. ... I try to fix mistakes I make.	○	○	○	○	○	○
23. ... I apologize if I hurt someone's feelings.	○	○	○	○	○	○
24. ... I feel like I have important responsibilities in my group.	○	○	○	○	○	○
25. ... I feel like I make important decisions in my group.	○	○	○	○	○	○
26. ... I feel like I contribute to my group's success.	○	○	○	○	○	○

(YOB-Pre)

For the following questions, think about the difficult problems you face when you are at home, in school, or participating in an activity. How do you respond when you face problems in your day-to-day life?

	False	Somewhat False	A Little True	Somewhat True	Mostly True	True
27. When I have a problem, I know the source.	○	○	○	○	○	○
28. When I have a problem, I look for the things that might be causing it.	○	○	○	○	○	○
29. When I have a problem, I stop and think about options before making a decision.	○	○	○	○	○	○
30. When I have a problem, I think about different ideas and then combine some to make the best decision.	○	○	○	○	○	○
31. When I have a problem, I choose a realistic plan.	○	○	○	○	○	○
32. When I have a problem, I make good choices about what to do.	○	○	○	○	○	○

Camp 2 Grow Youth Survey (Pretest) (cont.)

	False	Somewhat False	A Little True	Somewhat True	Mostly True	True
33. After dealing with a problem, I check to see if the problem has gotten better.	○	○	○	○	○	○
34. After dealing with a problem, I consider how it worked out.	○	○	○	○	○	○

(YOB PSC-Pre)

Camper Information

How old are you? _____

Gender (please circle):   Girl   Boy

Race/Ethnicity (please check):

_____ American Indian or Alaskan native   _____ Hispanic/Latino

_____ Asian   _____ Native Hawaiian/Pacific Islander

_____ Black/African American   _____ Biracial or multiracial

_____ Caucasian/White (non-Hispanic)

How many years have you attended this camp?_____

How many days will you be at this camp this summer? _____

What community or school activities have you participated in within the past 12 months? (check all that apply):

_____ sport team(s)   _____ church youth group

_____ drama/theater/music   _____ Scouts

_____ 4-H   _____ student council/government

_____ community organizations   _____ clubs (hobbies, debate, etc.)
(Sierra Club, Habitat for Humanity, etc.)

Have you volunteered at a community event during the past 12 months?

_____ Yes _____ No

If yes, what did you do?

Appendix C:
Camp 2 Grow Youth Survey (Posttest)

american CAMP association®

© American Camp Association 2011

CAMP 2 GROW END OF CAMP QUESTIONS

**PLEASE READ THE INSTRUCTIONS BELOW BEFORE
TURNING THE PAGE AND BEGINNING THE SURVEY.**

This survey will ask you about your experiences *while at camp*. Please take a moment to examine the sample questions below.

Please look at sample question A) below. The camper filling out this survey believes that the phrase "I enjoy playing team sports" is *somewhat true* for him and checks "Somewhat True."

	False	Somewhat False	A Little True	Somewhat True	Mostly True	True
A) I enjoy playing team sports.	○	○	○	✓	○	○

Let's look at one more example before we start. For question B) below, the camper indicated that the statement "I enjoy being outdoors" is *a little true* and checks "A Little True."

	False	Somewhat False	A Little True	Somewhat True	Mostly True	True
B) I enjoy being outdoors.	○	○	✓	○	○	○

As you begin, please think carefully about each of your answers. It is very important to be accurate. No answers are right or wrong, and everyone will have different answers. Please put down what you actually think for each question.

Do you understand the instructions? **If no, please ask for help.** If yes, turn the page and begin.

Your responses are important and will help us make camp better for future campers!

Camp 2 Grow Youth Survey (Posttest) (cont.)

For the following set of questions, think about the time you have spent at camp. Before each question, think to yourself, "After being involved in Camp 2 Grow at camp…"

	False	Somewhat False	A Little True	Somewhat True	Mostly True	True
1. I like being in nature.	○	○	○	○	○	○
2. I want to spend time outdoors.	○	○	○	○	○	○
3. I enjoy the freedom of being outside.	○	○	○	○	○	○
4. I am comfortable in the outdoors.	○	○	○	○	○	○
5. I feel connected to the natural environment.	○	○	○	○	○	○

(AFN-Post)

For the following set of questions, think about your time at camp and say to yourself, "After being involved in Camp 2 Grow at camp, when I participate in a group activity…"

	False	Somewhat False	A Little True	Somewhat True	Mostly True	True
6. … I can help my group be successful.	○	○	○	○	○	○
7. … I can help others succeed.	○	○	○	○	○	○
8. … I can support my group members even when they have decided to do something I do not want to do.	○	○	○	○	○	○
9. … I can appreciate opinions that are different from my own.	○	○	○	○	○	○
10. … I can place group goals above the things I want.	○	○	○	○	○	○
11. … I can cooperate with others.	○	○	○	○	○	○
12. … I can be helpful in a small group of kids my age.	○	○	○	○	○	○
13. … I can work well with other people in a small group.	○	○	○	○	○	○
14. … I need less help from adults.	○	○	○	○	○	○
15. … I can make decisions by myself.	○	○	○	○	○	○
16. … I can make decisions without adults helping me .	○	○	○	○	○	○
17. … I can take care of myself.	○	○	○	○	○	○

Camp 2 Grow Youth Survey (Posttest) (cont.)

	False	Somewhat False	A Little True	Somewhat True	Mostly True	True
18. ... I accept responsibility for my actions.	O	O	O	O	O	O
19. ... I own up to my mistakes.	O	O	O	O	O	O
20. ... I do not blame others for my mistakes.	O	O	O	O	O	O
21. ... I try to make things right if I mess something up.	O	O	O	O	O	O
22. ... I try to fix mistakes I make.	O	O	O	O	O	O
23. ... I apologize if I hurt someone's feelings.	O	O	O	O	O	O
24. ... I feel like I have important responsibilities in my group.	O	O	O	O	O	O
25. ... I feel like I make important decisions in my group.	O	O	O	O	O	O
26. ... I feel like I contribute to my group's success.	O	O	O	O	O	O

(YOB/EMP-Post)

For the following questions, think about what you have learned in the Camp 2 Grow program at camp. How do you respond when you face problems in your day-to-day life?

	False	Somewhat False	A Little True	Somewhat True	Mostly True	True
27. When I have a problem, I know the source.	O	O	O	O	O	O
28. When I have a problem, I look for the things that might be causing it.	O	O	O	O	O	O
29. When I have a problem, I stop and think about options before making a decision.	O	O	O	O	O	O
30. When I have a problem, I think about different ideas and then combine some to make the best decision.	O	O	O	O	O	O
31. When I have a problem, I choose a realistic plan.	O	O	O	O	O	O
32. When I have a problem, I make good choices about what to do.	O	O	O	O	O	O

	False	Somewhat False	A Little True	Somewhat True	Mostly True	True
33. After dealing with a problem, I check to see if the problem has gotten better.	○	○	○	○	○	○
34. After dealing with a problem, I consider how it worked out.	○	○	○	○	○	○

(YOB PSC-Post)

Appendix D:
Camp 2 Grow Parent Survey

1. Perceptions About Your Child

Please answer the following set of questions about your perceptions of your child since their return home from camp. Think of your child several months ago (prior to attending camp) and compare to what you notice today. There are no "right answers" so just respond based on your own observations.

1. Since returning from camp, my child seems:

	False	Somewhat False	A Little True	Somewhat True	Mostly True	True
more comfortable in the outdoors	○	○	○	○	○	○
more connected to the natural environment	○	○	○	○	○	○
to talk more about conservation practices like recycling,reducing pollution, etc.	○	○	○	○	○	○
to be more of a team player	○	○	○	○	○	○
more willing to accept leadership roles	○	○	○	○	○	○
more likely to take actions that support her/his beliefs	○	○	○	○	○	○
more independent	○	○	○	○	○	○
to be better at thinking through solutions to problems before taking action	○	○	○	○	○	○
to be confident in her/his decisions	○	○	○	○	○	○
more confident	○	○	○	○	○	○
more interested in issues facing our community	○	○	○	○	○	○
more interested in being involved in our community	○	○	○	○	○	○
more likely to talk positively about her/his leadership abilities	○	○	○	○	○	○
more interested in getting our family involved in outdoor nature activities	○	○	○	○	○	○

2. How do you think your child was influenced by her/his experience at camp this summer?

2. Your Child's Project

Please provide your perspective on the following questions about the implementation of your child's leadership action plan designed as a part of their camp experience.

Camp 2 Grow Parent Survey (cont.)

3. After your child returned home from camp, did she/he carry out a leadership project they had designed at camp?

○ Yes   ○ No   ○ Not sure

Other comments:

4. If your child carried out a leadership project, please answer the following question. My child:

	False	Somewhat False	A Little True	Somewhat True	Mostly True	True
discussed their action plan for the project with me	○	○	○	○	○	○
seemed excited about their action plan	○	○	○	○	○	○
involved our family/friends in the project	○	○	○	○	○	○
seemed comfortable in carrying out the project	○	○	○	○	○	○
Carried out the project successfully	○	○	○	○	○	○

Other (please specify)

3. Parent/Caregiver Information for Person Completing This Survey

5. Your child's initials and birth date (critical for matching your views with your camper's):
   Example: Mary Sue Jones, born May 26, 1998 would be: MSJ052698

6. Name of the camp your child attended:

Other (please specify)

Camp 2 Grow Parent Survey (cont.)

7. Role

   ○ Mother   ○ Father   ○ Other (please specify) _____

8. Your Education Level

   ○ Less than high school degree   ○ High school

   ○ Some college/technical school   ○ 2 year college/technical degree

   ○ 4 year college degree   ○ Postbaccalaureate study

9. Family Classification

   ○ Working class   ○ Middle class

   ○ Upper middle class   ○ Upper class

10. Did you ever go to camp as a child?

    ○ Yes   ○ No

11. Please share any other comments you would like for us to know about your child's camp experience.

4. Thank You for Your Help!

Appendix E:
Camp 2 Grow Staff Survey

1. Instructions

Please complete this survey after each lesson you conduct as a part of the leadership training program. Your feedback is critical to the improvement of the training and the lessons. Thanks for your help!

2. Staff Information

1. Camp: _____

2. Staff Member's Name: _____

3. Lesson #: _____

   Today's Lesson(s): _____ Leadership Lesson: _____

   If other (please specify) _____

4. How many minutes did you spend today implementing this lesson?
   - ○ <20 minutes
   - ○ 20-29 minutes
   - ○ 30-39 minutes
   - ○ 40-49 minutes
   - ○ 50-59 minutes
   - ○ 60-69 minutes
   - ○ 70 or more minutes

5. The amount of time for this lesson was:
   - ○ way too short
   - ○ a little short
   - ○ just right
   - ○ a little too long
   - ○ way too long

6. Approximately how much of the lesson were you able to cover in the time designated?
   - ○ 100%
   - ○ 75%
   - ○ 50%
   - ○ 25%
   - ○ <25%

7. You were able to implement the lesson as described in the curriculum:
   - ○ almost exactly as shown
   - ○ mostly as shown
   - ○ a little as shown
   - ○ not at all as shown

8. Based on what you observed in the campers, rate their reactions to the lesson:

interest in lesson   ○ High   ○ Medium   ○ Low

participation   ○ High   ○ Medium   ○ Low

9. Indicate your reactions to teaching this lesson:

Enjoyed   ○ High   ○ Medium   ○ Low

Frustrated   ○ High   ○ Medium   ○ Low

Satisfied (with your effort)   ○ High   ○ Medium   ○ Low

Interested   ○ High   ○ Medium   ○ Low

10. Approximate number of minutes campers spent reading/writing during (or related to) this lesson

  ○ <10 minutes   ○ 10-14 minutes   ○ 15-19 minutes

  ○ 20-29 minutes   ○ 30-39 minutes   ○ 40 or more minutes

11. Do you think this lesson should be kept as a part of the curriculum?

  ○ Yes   ○ No   ○ Maybe (please specify) _____

12. What would you change about this lesson to improve it?

13. What worked well in this lesson?

14. Considering the goal of teaching leadership in your camp, how well did this lesson fit?

  ○ Did not fit at all   ○ Fit a little bit

  ○ Fit ok   ○ Fit great

15. Please share any other perspectives about this lesson:

3. THANK YOU!!!

Appendix F:
Community Resources List

- American Farm Bureau Federation (http://www.fb.org)

- Audubon Society (www.audubon.org)

- Churches and other members of the faith-based community

- Civic organizations

- Colleges/universities

- Cooperation Extension System Offices (4-H, family/consumer sciences, agriculture/ natural resources) (www.csrees.usda.gov/Extension)

- Corporations

- Department of Conservation and Recreation

- Department of Forestry

- Middle and high schools (example: science teachers in applicable grades)

- NASA (www.nasa.gov/audience/forstudents/index.html)

- National FFA Organization – Living to Serve Program (https://www.ffa.org/programs/ grantsandscholarships/LivingtoServe/Pages/default.aspx#)

- National Park Service (www.nps.gov/index.htm)

- Nature Clubs for Families (www.childrenandnature.org/movement/naturalfamilies/ clubs)

- Nature Rocks (See the "Find Nature" map) (www.naturerocks.org)

- Outdoor clubs (examples: family nature clubs, birding, gardening, hiking, wildflowers, outdoor adventure, and many more)

- Planet Explore (www.planetexplore.com)

- Sierra Club (www.sierraclub.org)

- U.S. Fish & Wildlife Service (www.fws.gov)

- U.S. Forest Service (www.fs.fed.us)

Appendix G:
Resources for Nature-Focused Youth Programs

- *Affinity for Nature Scale*—Youth outcomes scale designed to measure whether a youth program experience helped a child become more emotionally attracted to nature. This scale is one of several available in the ACA's Youth Outcomes Battery, a set of age-appropriate youth surveys that have been tested in day and resident camps. (www.acacamps.org/research/youth-camp-outcomes-battery)

- *Camping Magazine articles related to Children and Nature*—A variety of articles in this ACA publication provide ideas for incorporating nature into your programs and operations. (www.acacamps.org/members/nature/aca_resources.php)

- *Children and Nature Network*—Created to encourage and support the people and organizations working to reconnect children with nature. C&NN is a national leader in the children-nature movement, and many resources can be found on its website. C&NN provides information on the Natural Families Network, the Natural Teachers Network, and the Natural Leaders Network. C&NN also provides research reports on the importance of nature for children. (www.childrenandnature.org)

- *Children's Outdoor Bill of Rights*—In 2007, California developed the first statewide outdoor children's bill of rights. Other states and organizations can adopt their own version of this popular document. (http://calroundtable.org/cobor.htm)

- *Connecting Children and Nature Online Course*—An online course for youth development professionals and the public developed by the ACA and the National Recreation and Park Association. Focuses on indoor syndrome and best practices for helping children to bond with nature and enjoy unstructured outdoor experiences. (www.acacamps.org/einstitute)

- *Green Spoken Here*—Program through which groups of children and adults (camp groups, youth groups, or families) can pledge to be active in environmental stewardship. (www.acacamps.org/members/nature/green_spoken_here.php)

- *Growing Up Wild*—Early childhood education program targeting children ages three through seven that builds on children's sense of wonder about nature and invites them to explore wildlife and the world (rooted out of Project WILD). (www.projectwild.org/growingupwild.htm)

- *iCARE*—Curriculum developed by the YMCA that provides nature-based activities structured around environmental awareness, appreciation, and action. iCARE environmental activities help kids understand the green "responsibility" character value by learning how things in nature work.
  (http://147.203.4.75/product_2185_detailed.htm)

- *Nature Circle Cards*—A "take it with you resource" developed by Hooked on Nature that makes it easy for anyone anywhere to create a circle experience for friends, family, neighbors, and coworkers. (www.hookedonnature.org/toolsforchange.html)

- *Nature Club for Families Toolkit*—A simple do-it-yourself guide developed by the Children Nature Network for families interested in creating nature clubs to get children outdoors. No fee. Little organization. Easy.
  (www.childrenandnature.org/downloads/NCFF_toolkit.pdf)

- *Nature Education Resources Web Page*—The American Camp Association has compiled a wide variety of nature education resources for camp and youth development professionals. (www.acacamps.org/nature-education-resources)

- *101 Nature Resources (Sanborn and Rundle, 2011)*—101 Nature Activities for Kids is a "one-stop shop" for those seeking a "perfect" and memorable nature activity for their group. Available through Healthy Learning. (www.healthylearning.com)

References

American Camp Association. (2011a). *2010 Camp 2 Grow Impact Report*. Unpublished Report. American Camp Association. Available at www.acacamps.org/camp2grow.

American Camp Association. (2011b). *Camp Demographics Export*. Unpublished Report. American Camp Association.

Arnold, H.E., Cohen, F.G., & Warner, A. (2009). Youth and environmental action: Perspectives of young environmental leaders on their formative influences. *Journal of Environmental Education, 40*(3), 27-36.

Arnold, M.E. (2006). Developing evaluation capacity in Extension 4-H field faculty: A framework for success. *American Journal of Evaluation, 27*, 257-269.

Benson, P., & Pittman, K. (2001). *Trends in Youth Development: Visions, Realities, and Challenges*. New York: Springer.

Bialeschki, M.D. (2009). *Journaling Tip Sheet*. American Camp Association.

Bialeschki, M.D., & Conn, M. (2011). Welcome to our world: Bridging youth development research in nonprofit and academic communities. *Journal of Research on Adolescence, 21*(1), 300-306.

Bialeschki, M.D., Henderson, K.A., & James, P.A. (2007). Camp experiences and developmental outcomes for youth. *Child and Adolescent Psychiatric Clinics of North America, 16*, 769-788.

Bird, M., Borba, J., Brenner, J., Brosnahan, A., Coutellier, C., George, J., Kong, L., Schmitt-McQuitty, L., Subramaniam, A., Thomas, J. (2008). *Beyond Evaluation: Findings From the California 4-H Camp Study*. Available at www.cyfernet.org.

Blanchard, K., & Cathy, S.T. (2002). *The Generosity Factor*. Grand Rapids, MI: Zondervan.

Bowden, B. (2001). *The Bowden Way, 50 Years of Leadership Wisdom*. Marietta, GA: Longstreet Press.

Browne, L., Garst, B., & Bialeschki, M.D. (2011). Engaging youth in environmental sustainability: Impact of the Camp 2 Grow program. *Journal of Park and Recreation Administration, 29*(3), 70-85.

Chan, J.C., McDermott, K.B., & Roediger, H.L. (2007). Retrieval-induced facilitation. *Journal of Experimental Psychology: General, 135*(4), 553-571.

Charles, C., & Louv, R. (2009). *Children's Nature Deficit: What We Know and Don't Know.* Sante Fe, NM: Children and Nature Network.

Chawla, L. (1999). Life paths into effective environmental action. *Journal of Environmental Education*, 31(1), 15-27.

Clay, B. (1999). *Career Development & Leadership: An Information Sourcebook for Leadership Training Activities.* Topeka, KS: Kansas Curriculum Center, Washburn University.

Connellan, T.K. (1988). *How To Grow People Into Self Starters.* Ann Arbor: The Achievement Institute.

Connors, R. (1998). *The Oz Principle: Getting Results Through Individual & Organizational Accountability.* New York: Prentice Hall.

DeGraaf, D., & Glover, J. (2003). Long-term impacts of working at an organized camp for seasonal staff. *Journal of Park and Recreation Administration,* 21(1), 1-20.

Eccles, J., & Gootman, J.A. (Eds.). (2002). *Community Programs to Promote Youth Development.* Washington, DC: National Academy Press.

Ellis, G., Sibthorp, J., & Bialeschki, M. D. (2007). *Development and Validation of a Camper Outcomes Battery,* pp. 106-109. NRPA Leisure Research Symposium. Indianapolis, IN.

Forsythe, K., Matysik, R., & Nelson, K. (2004). *Impact of the 4-H Camp Counseling Experience.* Madison: University of Wisconsin-Extension, Department of Youth Development.

Garst, B. (2010). From what to how: Targeting specific factors that influence outcomes. *Journal of Extension,* 48(6). Available at www.joe.org/joe/2010december/comm1.php.

Garst, B., Bialeschki, M.D., & Browne, L. (2010). *Camp 2 Grow Impact Report.* American Camp Association. Available at www.acacamps.org/sites/default/files/images/camp2grow/2010_Camp2Grow_Impact_Report.pdf.

Garst, B., & Chavez, C. (2010). Camp 2 Grow: Teaching leadership and environmental stewardship to New York City youth. *Camping Magazine.* American Camp Association.

Garst, B., & Johnson, J. (2005). Adolescent leadership skill development through residential 4-H camp counseling. *Journal of Extension,* 43(5). Available at www.joe.org/joe/2005october/rb5.php.

Hart, D., & Atkins, R. (2002). Civic competence in urban youth. *Applied Developmental Science*, 6(4), 227-236.

Henderson, K.A., Bialeschki, M.D., & James, P.A. (2007). Overview of camp research. *Child and Adolescent Psychiatric Clinics of North America,* 16, 755-767.

James, J.J. (2003). *The Threshold for Staff Transformation: An Ethnography of Girl Scout Camp Staff.* Available at http://acacamps.org/research/03symposium.pdf.

Johnson, S., & Blanchard, K. (1998). *Who Moved My Cheese? An Amazing Way to Deal With Change in Your Work and in Your Life.* New York: Putnam.

Kals, E., Schumacher, D., & Montada, L. (1999). Emotional affinity toward nature as a motivational basis to protect nature. *Environment and Behavior,* 31(2), 178-202.

Katzenbach, J., & Smith, D. (1993). The discipline of teams. *Harvard Business Review,* March–April, 111-120.

Keeter, S., Zukin, C., Andolina, M., & Jenkins, K., (2002). *The Civic and Political Health of the Nation: A Generational Portrait.* The Center for Information and Research on Civic Learning and Engagement.

Kellert, S.R. (2005). *Building for Life: Designing and Understanding the Human-Nature Connection.* Washington, DC: Island Press.

Koomey, J. (2001). *Turning Numbers Into Knowledge: Mastering the Art of Problem Solving.* Oakland: Analytics Press.

Lerner, R.M., Lerner, J.V., Almerigi, J., & Theokas, C. (2005). Positive youth development: A view of the issues. *Journal of Early Adolescence,* 25(1), 10-16.

Louv, R. (2005). *Last Child in the Woods: Saving Our Children From Nature-Deficit Disorder.* Chapel Hill: Algonquin Books.

Lyons, K.D. (2000). Personal investment as a predictor of camp counselor job performance. *Journal of Park and Recreation Administration,* 18(2), 21-36.

MacNeil, C.A. (2006). Bridging generations: Applying "adult" leadership theories to youth leadership development. *New Directions for Youth Development,* 109, 27-43.

Marshall, M. (2001). *Discipline Without Stress, Punishments or Rewards: How Facilitators and Parents Promote Responsibility & Learning.* New York: Piper Press.

Maxwell, J. (1984). *Your Road Map for Success.* Nashville: Thomas Nelson.

Maxwell, J. (1993). *Developing the Leader Within You.* Nashville: Thomas Nelson.

Maxwell, J. (2002). *The 17 Essential Laws of a Team Player.* Nashville: Thomas Nelson.

McKay, M., & Fanning, P. (2002). *Successful Problem Solving: A Workbook to Overcome the Four Core Beliefs That Keep You Stuck.* Oakland: Harbinger Publications.

Miller, J. (2001). QBQ! *The Question Behind the Question.* Denver: Denver Press.

Moore, R.C., & Cooper Marcus, C. (2008). Healthy planet, healthy children: Designing nature into the daily spaces of childhood. In S. Kellert, J.H. Heerwagen, & M. Mador (Eds.), *Biophilic Design: Theory, Science, and Practice.* Hoboken: John Wiley & Sons.

National FFA Organization. (2003). *Essential Learnings.* Indianapolis, IN: National FFA Organization.

National FFA Organization. (2004). *LifeKnowledge Online Leadership Curriculum.* National FFA Organization. Available at www.ffa.org/ffaresources/educators/lifeknowledge.

The Nature Conservancy. (2011). *Kids These Days: Why Is America's Youth Staying Indoors?* Available at www.nature.org/newsfeatures/kids-in-nature/kids-in-nature-poll.xml.

Ozier, L. (2010). Camp as educator: Lessons learned from history. *Camping Magazine.* American Camp Association. Available at www.acacamps.org/campmag/1009/camp-educator-lessons-learned-history.

Partnership for 21st Century Skills. (2011). *Framework for 21st Century Learning.* Partnership for 21st Century Skills. Available at www.p21.org/storage/documents/1.__p21_framework_2-pager.pdf.

Pittman, K.J., Irby, M., Tolman, J., Yohalem, N., & Ferber, T. (2003b). *Preventing Problems, Promoting Development, Encouraging Engagement: Competing Priorities or Inseparable Goals?* Based on Pittman, K., & Irby, M. (1996). *Preventing Problems or Promoting Development?* Washington, DC: The Forum for Youth Investment, Impact Strategies, Inc. Available at www.forumfyi.org.

Popov, K.L. (2000). *The Virtues Project Educator's Guide.* Torrance, CA: Jalmar Press.

Powell, G.M., Bixler, R.D., & Switzer, D.M. (2003). Perceptions of learning among new and returning seasonal camp staff. *Journal of Park and Recreation Administration,* 21(1), 61-74.

Reardon, M., & Derner, S. (2004). *Strategies for Great Teaching.* Chicago: Zephyr Press.

Rubinstein, J.S., Meyer, D.E., & Evans, J.E. (2001). Executive control of cognitive processes in task switching. *Journal of Experimental Psychology: Human Perception and Performance,* 27(4), 763-797.

Sibthorp, J. (2001). *Development and Validation of the Characteristics of the Experience Scale for Use in Adventure-Based Programming.* 2001 NRPA Leisure Research Symposium. Denver, CO.

Sibthorp, J. (2008). *Development and Validation of the Affinity for Nature Scale for Youth (technical report).* Martinsville, IN: American Camp Association.

Taylor, A.F., & Kuo, F.E. (2006). Is contact with nature important for healthy child development? State of the evidence. In Spencer, C. & Blades, M. (Eds.), *Children and Their Environments: Learning, Using and Designing Spaces,* pp. 124-158. New York: Cambridge University Press.

Thurber, C.A., Scanlin, M.A., Scheuler, L., & Henderson, K.A. (2007). Youth development outcomes of the camp experience: Evidence for multidimensional growth. *Journal of Youth & Adolescence,* 36, 241-254.

Toupence, R.H., & Townsend, C.D. (2000). Leadership development and youth camping: Determining a relationship. In L.A. Stringer, L.I. McAvoy, & A.B. Young (Eds.), *Coalition for Education in the Outdoors Fifth Biennial Research Symposium Proceedings,* pp. 82-88. Cortland, NY: Coalition of Education in the Outdoors.

Trudeau, F., & Shephard, R.J. (2008). Physical education, school physical activity, school sports and academic performance. *International Journal of Behavioral Nutrition and Physical Activity,* 5(1), 1-12.

Vinal, W.G. (1935). The value of nature leadership in camp as training for the teaching of elementary science. *Science Education,* 19(1), 16-19.

Willis, J. (2008). Brain-based teaching strategies for improving students' memory, learning, and test-taking success. *Childhood Education,* 83(5), 310-316.

Yohalem, N., & Martin, S. (2007). Building the evidence base for youth engagement: Reflections on youth & democracy. *Journal of Community Psychology,* 35(6), 807-810.

About the Authors

Barry A. Garst, Ph.D., is the director of Program Development and Research Application with the American Camp Association and an adjunct professor in the Department of Agricultural and Extension Education at Virginia Tech.

A native of Virginia, Barry attended camp from age 8 through 21, serving in every role, including camper, counselor-in-training, teen counselor, staff member, and volunteer adult leader. His professional career began in mental health services in North Carolina, where he worked as a counselor in wilderness, school, home, and clinical settings. He joined the faculty at Virginia Tech in 1998—first as the director of programming for a large residential camp and conference center and then as an assistant professor of youth development from 2001 through 2007. Barry joined the American Camp Association in 2007 and now provides leadership to national projects across research, education, and business development.

Barry graduated from Virginia Tech with a B.S. in psychology, completed his M.S. degree at Arizona State University in recreation administration, and earned a Ph.D. from Virginia Tech in the human dimensions of forestry. Barry frequently publishes and presents in the areas of youth development, program evaluation, risk management, volunteer development, research trends, and the human values of nature. Barry resides in Salem, Virginia, with his wife Stephanie and daughters Savannah and Laurel.

Christine P. White, M.S., is the director of the Educational Programs Division with the National FFA Organization. Christine joined the organization in 2006 as an education specialist. Her role is to provide leadership and direction for the educational programs that are delivered to the more than 540,000 FFA members nationwide.

Christine's professional career began in 1999 as an agricultural educator and FFA advisor. Christine spent seven years teaching agricultural education in Florida and Virginia.

Christine graduated from the Delaware Valley College of Science and Agriculture, earning a B.S. in education with a concentration in agriculture. She earned her M.S. degree from Capella University in educational leadership and administration. Christine resides in Whitestown, Indiana, with her husband David and son Sebastian.